CURIOUS HABITS

Why we do what we do
and how to change

CURIOUS HABITS

LUKE MATHERS

MAJOR
STREET

MAJOR
STREET

First published in 2022 by Major Street Publishing Pty Ltd
info@majorstreet.com.au | +61 421 707 983 | majorstreet.com.au

A catalogue record for this book is available
from the National Library of Australia

Printed book ISBN: 978-1-922611-42-0
Ebook ISBN: 978-1-922611-43-7

Cover design by Typography Studio
Internal design by Production Works

10 9 8 7 6 5 4 3 2 1

Contents

Preface

'The reasonable man adapts himself to the world:
the unreasonable one persists in trying to adapt the world
to himself. Therefore all progress depends on the
unreasonable man.'
– George Bernard Shaw

Dave was always the angry kid. He liked being thought of as a bit of a psycho.

As a 12-year-old, he loved baseball and played catcher. He was a skinny blond kid with a sideways snarl, and anyone who rounded third base had to get past him. Whether the ball was close or not, he would drop his bony prepubescent shoulder into anyone brave enough to head for home plate. He was the psycho catcher and his team loved him for it. He was *their* psycho!

Even as a kid, Dave was disagreeable, rebellious and a bit of a turd. He was a shit-stirrer; he was unreasonable, and he kind of liked that.

His father was an alcoholic who left his family when Dave was only four years old. His two sisters were 18 and 15 years older than him and were more like aunties than sisters. The family were Jehovah's Witnesses, but it is hard to imagine Dave with a shirt and tie going door to door with a bag full of Bibles and leaflets trying to convert any unsuspecting heathen.

Dave was going to change the world. He didn't know how, but he was angry enough, determined enough and certainly unreasonable enough to make something happen.

It was the late '70s, and teenage Dave was looking for other ways to vent his anger. After baseball, he found heavy metal. Big hair, angry guitars and a sound that could make your ears bleed. With a guitar in hand, Dave had found his calling and it was like a hand in a glove.

When his parents divorced, Dave and his sisters moved around a lot in an attempt to dodge his pissed-off father (the apple doesn't fall far from the tree). He moved out of home at 15 and could only afford to rent an apartment by selling drugs. One of his customers worked at a record store and would swap vinyl for drugs in a fortuitous exchange of one vice for another. Dave ended up with a massive collection of Iron Maiden, AC/DC and Judas Priest and would have really annoyed any unsuspecting neighbour who had the misfortune of living next door.

As the '80s came around, Dave joined a band. That band fell apart, so Dave answered a newspaper ad to join another band and was accepted. He was still angry, but the anger fuelled his guitar sound. The band started to record its debut album.

Musically, everything sounded fantastic, but Dave's disagreeable nature was taking its toll. One day in 1983, the band had finally had enough of their talented but angry guitarist. He got kicked out of the band, dumped at the Greyhound bus station and sent home. Fuming, he wrote songs and vowed to 'show them'. As soon as he got back home to San Francisco, he started a new band that was going to be huge.

His drive, passion and disagreeable nature paid off. His new band went on to sell 25 million albums and sell out stadiums around the world, and is considered one of the top heavy metal bands of all time.

Dave's full name is Dave Mustaine. His band is Megadeth.

Anger helped Dave become a good thrash metal guitarist. It helped him write songs that appealed to aggro teenagers in the '80s and '90s. Being aggressive, angry and disagreeable helped with a lot of things… until it didn't.

You'd think he'd be happy, but the booze, addiction, anger and aggression continued. The angry thought habits Dave had hammered into place over the years gave him a messed up, misguided idea that if he became really successful, he'd be joyful and happy. But he wasn't.

Harvard positive psychology scholar Shawn Achor calls this 'pushing happiness over the cognitive horizon'. We all do it:

- 'If I have the biggest thrash metal band in the world, then I'll be happy.'
- 'If I can pay the rent this month, then I'll be happy.'
- 'If I can get this piece of Kung Pao chicken out of my teeth, then I'll be happy.'
- 'If I can buy a seventh Ferrari, then I'll be happy.'

Putting off happiness until we've mastered or achieved something is a curious habit. It doesn't work, but we do it anyway.

By anyone's standards, Megadeth was successful. There's only one problem: the band Dave Mustaine got kicked out of in 1983 was Metallica, which went on to sell 250 million records and become the biggest metal band of all time. Success is relative and, for the angry Mr Mustaine, his benchmark was, unfortunately, the biggest band in town.

Former US President Theodore Roosevelt called comparison 'the thief of joy'. The Megadeth frontman found very little lasting joy for many years. His default habit was to look for pleasure in booze, drugs and massive parties. Any joy to be had was lost in a haze of cocaine or drowned in alcohol. His curious habit of being angry was always there, lurking in the background, waiting to rain on the parade of his success.

Dave's problem? He never got curious about his habits.

for running, catching and kicking will be really strong, while those associated with reading will have less brain space dedicated to them. It may not be the complete lobotomy of the sea squirt, but our brains shape themselves to what we habitually do.

Unlike the sea squirt's brain, human brains are made up of 86 billion neurons with 100 trillion links to other nerve cells. They're a complex bit of kit that scientists are only just starting to understand. One thing we do know is that the big, grey ball of jelly that we all have in our heads is a fuel guzzler. Your brain accounts for about 2 percent of your body weight but takes up around 20 percent of your energy needs. It's an expensive piece of equipment, and evolution wouldn't put up with that unless there was an upside.

We evolved in an environment without 7-Eleven, McDonald's or cheese nachos. Food was scarce and finding it took a lot of effort. A big, expensive brain would be a liability unless it helped us move, stay safe, connect with other people and find food. A large chunk of our brains is dedicated to those four motivating factors. Evolutionary biologists refer to the four Fs of motivation: fighting, fleeing, food and… reproduction. To save energy, our brains run partly on auto-pilot – driven by the four Fs.

The four Fs served us well for thousands of years. However, as our environment has become more plentiful, the four Fs are starting to F with us. Obesity, heart disease, stress, auto-immune diseases and cancer are rampant due to us not being deliberate with our intake, our energy or how we spend our time. The four Fs are useful, but without direction they can lead to some terrible outcomes. The problem is, they have a bias for short-term safety (or pleasure) and don't give a damn about your long-term plans.

We've allowed the four Fs to drive the ship without a compass for too long. Our habits – designed to help us avoid pain, seek pleasure and save energy – have been good to get us here, but we need to get and '90s. Being aggressive, angry and disagreeable helped with a lot of things… until it didn't.

You'd think he'd be happy, but the booze, addiction, anger and aggression continued. The angry thought habits Dave had hammered into place over the years gave him a messed up, misguided idea that if he became really successful, he'd be joyful and happy. But he wasn't.

Harvard positive psychology scholar Shawn Achor calls this 'pushing happiness over the cognitive horizon'. We all do it:

- 'If I have the biggest thrash metal band in the world, then I'll be happy.'
- 'If I can pay the rent this month, then I'll be happy.'
- 'If I can get this piece of Kung Pao chicken out of my teeth, then I'll be happy.'
- 'If I can buy a seventh Ferrari, then I'll be happy.'

Putting off happiness until we've mastered or achieved something is a curious habit. It doesn't work, but we do it anyway.

By anyone's standards, Megadeth was successful. There's only one problem: the band Dave Mustaine got kicked out of in 1983 was Metallica, which went on to sell 250 million records and become the biggest metal band of all time. Success is relative and, for the angry Mr Mustaine, his benchmark was, unfortunately, the biggest band in town.

Former US President Theodore Roosevelt called comparison 'the thief of joy'. The Megadeth frontman found very little lasting joy for many years. His default habit was to look for pleasure in booze, drugs and massive parties. Any joy to be had was lost in a haze of cocaine or drowned in alcohol. His curious habit of being angry was always there, lurking in the background, waiting to rain on the parade of his success.

Dave's problem? He never got curious about his habits.

Introduction

'I have no special talents. I am only passionately curious.'
– Albert Einstein

The sea squirt has a pretty small brain. A few thousand neurons are all it needs to avoid danger and find a nice place to settle down. It moves away from toxins and towards food and safety. Once it's found a good spot, it settles in – and by that I mean it settles in *permanently*. We know this because the sea squirt then digests its own brain. Yeah, you read that right. It settles down on the sea floor and proceeds to eat its own cerebrum. If you don't need to move, you don't need a brain.

I once told this story during a workshop I was running with a local city council and they were positive they had a few departments made up entirely of sea squirts.

It may seem strange to start a book about curious habits with a story of a marine slug, but you and I have a few things in common with these intriguing little fellas. We naturally move towards things that feel good and away from threats. We crave safety and try to save energy. As children, we even eat our own brains. Maybe not in the same dramatic fashion as our sea squirt friends, but we do go through a complex stage of development that reinforces brain areas that are being used a lot and prunes circuits that aren't being utilised. If, as a kid, you play a lot of football and hate reading, your circuits for running, catching and kicking will be really strong, while those associated with reading will have less brain space dedicated to them. It may not be the complete lobotomy of the sea squirt, but our brains shape themselves to what we habitually do.

Unlike the sea squirt's brain, human brains are made up of 86 billion neurons with 100 trillion links to other nerve cells. They're a complex bit of kit that scientists are only just starting to understand. One thing we do know is that the big, grey ball of jelly that we all have in our heads is a fuel guzzler. Your brain accounts for about 2 percent of your body weight but takes up around 20 percent of your energy needs. It's an expensive piece of equipment, and evolution wouldn't put up with that unless there was an upside.

We evolved in an environment without 7-Eleven, McDonald's or cheese nachos. Food was scarce and finding it took a lot of effort. A big, expensive brain would be a liability unless it helped us move, stay safe, connect with other people and find food. A large chunk of our brains is dedicated to those four motivating factors. Evolutionary biologists refer to the four Fs of motivation: fighting, fleeing, food and… reproduction. To save energy, our brains run partly on auto-pilot – driven by the four Fs.

The four Fs served us well for thousands of years. However, as our environment has become more plentiful, the four Fs are starting to F with us. Obesity, heart disease, stress, auto-immune diseases and cancer are rampant due to us not being deliberate with our intake, our energy or how we spend our time. The four Fs are useful, but without direction they can lead to some terrible outcomes. The problem is, they have a bias for short-term safety (or pleasure) and don't give a damn about your long-term plans.

We've allowed the four Fs to drive the ship without a compass for too long. Our habits – designed to help us avoid pain, seek pleasure and save energy – have been good to get us here, but we need to get curious about them if we want to thrive in a world with electric cars, iPhones, wi-fi and Uber Eats. As author Marshall Goldsmith says, 'What got you here won't get you there'.

Our world is safer and less violent. Medicine has improved out of sight, and diseases are causing less suffering than any time in history (COVID-19 excepted). But despite this, we are the most addicted, distracted, obese, in-debt, medicated, anxious, depressed and messed up group of adults the Western world has ever known.

But we don't have to be. Let's get curious.

Some is good, more is better

In my late twenties, I had a curious habit of working like a madman and trying to party like a rock star. I was an optometrist and spent my days helping people see better, and my nights and weekends seeing how much fun I could squeeze into whatever time there was leftover.

I was running my first business: the Specsavers store in the sleepy little town of Crawley, West Sussex, England. The town was rapidly developed in the postwar period and was full of square brick, soulless buildings that housed people who were way more fun than their ugly-duckling town suggested. The store was a 'dog with fleas' when I took it over: exhausted, unappreciated staff giving shit service, with really bad systems and leaders who only cared about how much money they made (more about this curious habit later). The store was losing money, and the wannabe-rich owners wanted out.

I realised that lots of people were coming through the door; the problem was, they weren't being looked after very well. The staff had good intentions, but good intentions with poor systems only lead to frustration and burnout.

My first job on day one was to fire the manager. She was nicknamed 'the rottweiler', and every staff member was petrified of doing something wrong and getting chewed out by the boss. Micromanaging is a curious habit, and she was great at it. She had to go.

We got curious about our systems, and I encouraged the staff to try new ways of doing things. It turns out they had lots of great ideas; all they needed was the safety to express them and the trust that it was OK to try something new, even if it failed.

The crew was working hard, and their new systems, along with increased autonomy and appreciation, gave them energy to burn. Before long, we had created a beast of a business and our financial worries were over. The place was booming.

At that time, my default way of doing things was 'some is good, more is better'. I applied this to work, partying, beer, food, exercise and anything I enjoyed. I didn't apply it to self-care, meditation or relaxation. I was living the Bon Jovi principle of living while you're alive and sleeping when you're dead. Like all curious habits, it worked until it didn't.

After four years of long work hours, English winters (which totally suck) and lots of partying, I was feeling burnt out and longing to move back to Australia. I sold the goose that laid the golden egg and moved home. Cashed up, I bought a house, invested the rest and essentially retired (for the first time). I was 31 years old. (Cue fireworks, streamers and balloons!)

It sounds awesome, doesn't it? I didn't have to work anymore, after slogging away and working my butt off for many years. The struggle to balance earning, spending and ambition was finally over. I'd made it to the top of my mountain. It was like I had won the lottery. I got my golf handicap down to six, I went surfing most days, and a new baby arriving was the cherry on the top of the cake of my new utopia life.

You can feel a 'but' coming, can't you? Of course, you can! Be careful what you wish for – you might just get it.

About 18 months later, I started to get a bit agitated, disillusioned and bored. My friends were all doing amazing things with their businesses, feeling great about the directions they were headed in and the contributions they were making to the world. I was attaching my self-worth to my golf score or how well I surfed. If you've ever seen me putt or surf, you'll realise this is a recipe for disaster.

Is the world a better place because you are in it? If the answer is 'no', think again. If the answer is still 'no', do something positive and contribute.

If you aren't contributing, your self-worth will nosedive, and little things will become big worries. We humans need challenges in our lives. If you don't have a challenge that contributes to the greater good, you start creating dramas and causing problems just to have something to overcome.

There is an African proverb that says, 'A child who is not embraced by the village will burn it down to feel its warmth'. To be fully embraced by your village, you need to contribute. Without a sense of contribution, you'll start to develop curious habits that burn down your life. You'll find dramas where there are none, create problems that don't need to be created and do things 'just to feel the heat'. That's a really curious habit.

That's what happened to me. I had spent four years building a business and contributing to my team, and suddenly it was all over. The relief and euphoria of not having to work was ridiculously fleeting. Before long, my mood was in the gutter. Without a purpose and the stress of striving to improve, my days were blurring into each other, with no challenges to punctuate the weeks.

When life is out of balance, we long for the other extreme. Too busy? All we want to do is chill. Bored? Let's get fired up. The grass is always greener. This can be destructive unless we get curious about what we feel, think and do. Curiosity lets us find joy by bouncing deliberately from one side of the fence to the other. When we master this, we get to chow down on the greenest grass and embrace life with the presence and acceptance that comes with being truly curious.

Curiosity: the superpower to change

There are hundreds of books about habits – atomic habits, tiny habits and habits of highly effective people (there are seven of those). There are books on 'how to change', 'the power of habit' and understanding 'the craving mind'. Great philosophers, writers, scientists and scholars have written about habits since Moses found the ten habits that won't piss off God.

This book is different. It draws from the collective wisdom – every-thing from evolutionary biology and neuroscience to ancient wisdom, Stoic philosophy and Instagram – and looks at habits through the lens of curiosity, not scarcity.

Have you ever stopped after doing something you've done a hundred times and thought, 'Why the hell do I do that?'

That's a curious habit.

A curious habit is anything you feel, think or do where your default no longer helps.

Your curious habits served a purpose at some point. They helped you deal with life as a messy human. But over time, they've become redundant (or worse, destructive). Because you're human – and you crave safety and pleasure, just like the sea squirt – your curious habits are running your life. Left unchecked, they may have led you away from the very things that make life joyful and meaningful.

If you're like most people, you probably blame yourself for the curious habits you've unconsciously developed. But what if you could look at your habits from a place of love and acceptance instead? What if you knew that change is possible if you *want* to change?

The modern world tells us that we are not good enough – that we need to be richer, thinner and more successful to be worthy humans. Instead, let's embrace the joy of growth from a place of love (of ourselves and others).

A curious habit is not so much unconscious as unexamined, and this examination is within your power to do.

When you get curious about your habits, your default position becomes 'I *want* to change, because I know I have more to offer', rather than 'I *have* to change, because I'm not good enough'. You approach change from a place of positivity and striving. This is when lasting change happens.

I'd love to say that I'm writing this book because I have mastered all my habits. If that were true, I'd be sporting a sixpack and sailing on my superyacht, and Tony Robbins would be coming to me for advice. This book is not about *perfect*. If it was, I wouldn't be the right author. I procrastinate. I struggle with my weight and wrestle with imposter syndrome. But it's still great being me.

There are things we all want to change about ourselves and what we do. Unfortunately, the default method of change usually starts with 'I'm not enough'. Most people try to change their habits from a place of scarcity and lack. This book will make you get curious about what you do and get your habits to work for you, rather than continuing your constant battle with failing willpower. My first book, *Stress Teflon*, was about the positive side of stress. This book is about taking the stress out of change. We are going to learn to change because we *want* to, not because we have to.

It's about how to change your thought habits – your beliefs and the stories you tell yourself – so you can deal with your shit and live a more authentic life. It's about making decisions rather than relying on defaults. It's about discovering the joy of doing things on purpose and for the right reasons (that are your own), and becoming aware of when you are on autopilot. It's about choosing deliberate habits that are aligned with who you want to be. It's about knowing that emotion drives action, and having the power to put space between your emotional reactions and your deliberate behaviours so you can make better choices.

In the words of Walt Whitman (and Ted Lasso), 'Be curious – not judgemental'.

Finding your 'why' (without vomiting in your mouth)

Self-help gurus tell us we need to find our 'why'. There are thousands of 'live a life of purpose' evangelists who will teach you how to discover life's answers for three easy payments of $49.95. This type of self-help speak makes a lot of people (including me) feel like they want to vomit in their mouths.

Unfortunately, finding your 'why' is really important. Unless you have a bigger, better reason driving your actions, it is impossible to sustain motivation and commitment. The problem is, a lot of self-help bullshit is condescending, blames the victim and uses guilt and scarcity to drive change. If you tell me I 'have to' do something, my instant reaction is to say 'Get lost'. Psychologists call the extreme version of this 'object defiance disorder', and I think that even the most agreeable people have a bit of defiance in them. Lasting change happens when we 'want to' do something because it aligns with our values and goals.

In this book, we are going to use curiosity to find exactly what our values are and uncover 'why' we do what we do. My aim is to do it without being preachy or prescriptive. You won't find any buzzwords like 'pivot', 'circle back' or 'synergy', or any language that makes you feel like you've just joined a cult.

Everyone has a different appreciation of and tolerance for nerdy science stuff. There are a million books that go super-deep into the science of habits. I'm going to draw on a bunch of them and give you some tools to help you get curious about change without making you feel like you just stepped into a neuroscience masterclass.

Getting curious about what motivates you is a great way to get shit done and enjoy doing it. It's much easier to commit to something you *want* to do than something you *have* to do to fit in with someone else's idea of what's important.

You're a diamond

My friend Michael DeSanti runs a men's coaching group called Find Your Tribe. He says: 'You are a diamond that is covered in shit'.

Capitalism tells us that diamonds are good, and we need to go out and get more diamonds. Mike's view is, **'Why don't we just wipe the shit off?'**

Getting curious and deliberate about your habits means discarding the stuff that isn't in line with your best self. Often subtraction is easier and more effective than addition; getting curious allows you to do both, regardless of your mathematical skillset. It's about finding harmony within yourself. As Mahatma Gandhi said: **'Happiness is when what you think, what you say, and what you do are in harmony'**.

When you scrape off the shit, you can show up as the better version of you that was there all along. You can direct your energy towards what I call your 'identity goals': characteristics that align with your 'why' and that you want to cultivate. Identity goals are intrinsic, intentional and infinite. If you get them right, they act as a north star, guiding you to be deliberate with your decisions and defaults.

To get rid of the shit, you have to learn how to get comfortable with discomfort. I think of this as a software upgrade that's designed to overcome your outdated (sea squirt) hardware. Human hardware has an evolutionarily outdated, obsolete and often unhelpful reward system. This messed-up system was great when we were chasing woolly mammoths around, but it doesn't work so well now. It leads to addiction and other behaviours that take you further and further away from who you want to be.

Getting comfortable with discomfort is necessary if you want to address your curious habits.

We're all looking for answers – this book is about asking questions

You want to know why your finances are down the toilet; why you can't find work-life balance (spoiler alert: it's always fleeting); why motivation eludes you, even when you really, *really* want something. You want to find the answers to better health, lower body fat and increased fitness. Maybe you want to find out why your relationships aren't working, and discover the secrets that unlock performance and happiness. None of these questions have hard-and-fast answers. Everybody is different, and what works for one person might be a disaster for another.

You know what *does* work for all of us, though? Curiosity.

This book will help you look at the things you do, and get curious about what you're getting out of them and how you can do things differently. Better.

We will look at curious habits around health and wealth, love and life, business and pleasure. I'll share some stories, sprinkle in some science, add some clumsy metaphors and overshare a bit of personal experience.

This book is not about how to *do* anything. It's about how to be curious. It's about always having options and being deliberate while looking at habit change from a place of thriving acceptance – not from the swamp of scarcity.

It's about living with more curiosity; less judgement. More bravery; less fear. More vulnerability; less perfection. More acceptance; less scarcity.

Are you curious? Let's jump in.

PART I

GET CURIOUS ABOUT HABITS

Before we start our deep dive into the most common and problematic curious habits, let's first learn why curious habits are so gnarly and persistent. We'll look at our human brains and why they're ill equipped to make good decisions; how addiction takes hold and can be so hard to break; and why it can be so bloody hard to change, even when you know your habits no longer serve you. You'll learn how to turn your triggers into cues to get curious, and change your default habit loops into deliberate habits that make your life better.

Are you curious? Let's rip in.

Chapter 1

You are a bundle of habits

'We are mere bundles of habits.'
– William James

A concerned father was worried about his son's bad habits. He sought counsel from a wise old man. The old man met the boy and took him out for a stroll. They walked into the woods, and the old man showed the boy a small weed and asked him to pull it out. The boy did so with ease, and they walked on.

The old man then asked the boy to pull out a small plant. The boy did that too, with a little more effort. As they walked, the old man asked the boy to pull out another weed, which he did. Next was a small bush, which the boy managed to pull out with a bit of a struggle.

Finally, the old man showed the boy a bigger tree and asked him to pull it out. The boy failed to pull it out even after trying several times in different ways.

The old man looked at the boy, smiled and said, 'So is the case with habits, good or bad'.

We all have habits – some that help and some that don't – and if William James is right (and I suspect he is), our habits become a big part of who we are. Habits are the things we do that don't take much thought. They are our defaults. Research suggests that anything from 40 to 70 percent of the things we do are habitual.

There is an old saying – often (wrongly) attributed to Aristotle – that says, 'We are what we repeatedly do'. Our habits become our identity. If you exercise every day, you become a fit person. If you have good habits with money, you become a wealthy person. If you have a habit of appreciating the good things in your life, you become a grateful person. If you only notice the negative, dark side of life and have a habit of being constantly pessimistic about everything, you become a miserable bastard. What we repeatedly feel, think and do drives our habits, and those habits form who we are.

None of our habits are permanent. If we get curious and want to change them, we can. If we want to change how we look at our habits, we can do that too.

The tree in the parable that opens this chapter could provide beautiful shade for a picnic. We should be glad the kid with the bad habits couldn't pull it out. If we do want to get rid of the tree, though, curiosity is like a chainsaw, and we can chop that sucker down branch by branch and build a log cabin.

Getting curious about habits and how they work can allow us to shape our health, happiness, businesses and who we want to be.

Dog spit and dancing pigeons

Humans have been curious about habits for centuries. By the early 20th century, scientists were starting to work out how little conscious thought is behind lots of the things we do. Russian dog-spit guru Ivan Pavlov discovered that if he rang a bell before feeding his dogs, he could get them to salivate by ringing the bell even if there was no food nearby. Walk past a bakery and smell chocolate-chip cookies coming out of the oven, and you'll see that we are not that different from

Pavlov's dribbling mutts. Our brains are prediction machines: we love a good pattern and search for signs that help prepare us for what's coming next.

Around the same time as Pavlov was getting dogs to drool to the sound of bells ringing, Columbia University professor Edward Thorndike started to look at how we learn, how habits form and how to change them. In the late 19th century he was one of the first to describe the habit loop, shown in Figure 1.1.

Figure 1.1: The habit loop

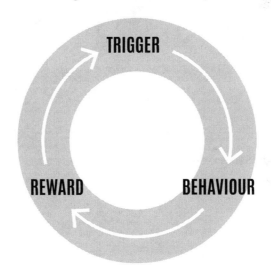

Thorndike described the 'Law of effect', which stated that any behaviour that is followed by pleasant consequences is likely to be repeated, and any behaviour followed by unpleasant consequences is likely to be stopped.

In the 1940s and '50s, along came B.F. Skinner and the behaviourists. This group of brain boffins did a bunch of experiments with animals to work out why they did the things they did. It turns out, the sea squirt was not on its own: mice, pigeons and dogs all move towards pleasure and away from pain.

One of the most cited, repeated and famous experiments of the 20th century involved Skinner's box: a contraption Skinner invented to study animal behaviour in a controlled environment. This box was set up to give rewards or punishments for different actions. Skinner and the other behaviourists discovered they could get animals to demonstrate a behaviour (like tapping a lever) by offering them a consistent reward (like tasty treats). Pigeons learned really quickly that if they tapped a lever inside the box, they would get some seed. He noticed that the animals quickly developed a habitual response to being in the box. Get in the box, tap the lever and chow down. You beauty! By finding the right rewards, these behaviour geeks could get pigeons to dance.

In one mean-spirited version of the box, the floor was electrified and rats had to press a certain button to stop being zapped. This worked in the same way. Demonstrating the behaviour to take away the bad thing was a good motivator for behaviour change as well. Who would have thought? If you zapped the floor of a Skinner box every time a rat pressed a certain button, it's not hard to imagine that the rat won't press that thing again. Getting zapped sucks!

Skinner called this 'operant conditioning'. Addiction specialist and mindfulness-based behaviour change guru Dr Judson Brewer calls it **'reward-based learning'**. If something is good, remember how you got it, and next time you see that option again, take it. All of this goes back to the motivators we talked about earlier: avoid pain, seek pleasure and save energy. It's sea squirt habits 101.

As Pavlov discovered, brains are prediction machines – even really small brains like those of the sea squirt and pigeon. Not only do these animals avoid pain and seek pleasure, they can even predict whether they will like something or not. Skinner noted that animals could predict when good things were going to happen and put themselves in a place to take advantage of them. It sounds a bit like the vultures circling the dehydrated and starving desert explorer: the vultures can tell he's struggling and predict that a feed is imminent.

This is when we start to get curious about habits, because once a habit is established you can remove the reward and people will still do the habit. Pavlov noticed that the bell ringing got the dogs drooling even when there was no chance they were going to get fed. Scientists call this type of habit 'reward invariant'. It means you'll do the habitual thing whether you get the reward or not.

Consider smoking – a curious habit if ever there was one. If you're a smoker, you probably started when you were a teenager, and it was a way to feel rebellious and grown-up, and connect with the other rebellious and grown-up cool kids. It made you feel part of a group, and that is a stronger attraction than the negative consequences of coughing up a lung and smelling like an ashtray. Nicotine threw in a little feel-good factor and, eventually, you started to get addicted to the nicotine and feel uncomfortable if you didn't have it.

Years later, the cool kids are gone. Smoking is no longer a way to connect with your tribe – it actually has the opposite effect, because you need to go outside to suck on your stinky little filter-tipped cancer stick. The original reward – connection – is gone, but the habit continues. This is where the 'save energy' part comes in. Once a habit is established, the brain pathways are laid down and you do the habit regardless of the reward. The habit becomes reward invariant.

Smoking is an interesting one because the chemical addiction adds an additional layer of compulsion. Depriving the addicted brain of its drug feels uncomfortable, and having a ciggie removes the discomfort. Next time you feel the discomfort of nicotine withdrawal, you know what will make you feel better, and you spark up another coffin nail.

But reward invariance works even for those habits that don't involve chemical ingestion. Some people are addicted to worrying – the new parent sees worrying about their baby as a sign they are a good, caring parent. Three decades later, there is very little reward in worrying about their middle-aged son, but they continue to do it anyway. Reward invariant!

Who's driving this thing?

Autopilot can be a great thing. Airline travel is exponentially safer thanks to advances in autopilot technology, which has saved thousands of lives by eliminating human error. The problem arises when you stay on autopilot even when you are heading in the wrong direction.

Getting curious about your habits is like realigning your autopilot so that what you do and where you want to go match.

If you have read my first book, *Stress Teflon*, you'll know that I have a great respect for evolutionary biology. We do stuff because cavemen did stuff. The original title of *Stress Teflon* was *The Caveman Advantage*. I believed then and still believe now that if you can understand why your body evolved to do certain things, you can use that knowledge to make changes to better navigate your world today. Being chased by prehistoric tigers may seem a long way from having your Facebook business account frozen, but your old-school, analogue physiology didn't get the email, doesn't have a computer and probably can't read. To your brain and body, the threats feel similar.

If you want to get curious about your habits, you need to venture back to prehistoric times and get an understanding of the hardware that kept humans alive 10,000 years ago – and the fact that those systems are still inside you today. A lot of our curious habits are remnants of behaviours that were essential to keep us alive back then – they just aren't helping now. It takes thousands of years for our bodies to evolve, but the world today is vastly different to what it was as little as 20 years ago. Our biology, our hardware, can't keep up with the changes in our environment.

For the majority of human existence, we have lived in an instant gratification environment. Consider hunter-gatherers on the plains of the Serengeti. They had three motivators to drive their action:

1. Avoid pain.
2. Seek pleasure.
3. Save energy.

These three motivators help us form our default habits. They are what we do in 'sea squirt mode', when our priority is what's happening *now*. Instant gratification is our default; it's all about safety and comfort *now*. There wasn't a lot of long-term planning going on 10,000 years ago. The most important thing was to stay alive. In an environment with sabre-toothed tigers, lions and big-arse woolly mammoths, staying alive was not so easy. Not getting killed too young was an evolutionary advantage, and the cavemen who were good at staying alive were those who passed their genes onto us.

Avoiding pain

As a personality trait, being negative is a bit like being the neglected middle kid with poor personal hygiene: no one wants this trait or wants to be around people who have it. The problem is, we are all genetically predisposed to being negative: the dominant, overriding driver in sea squirt mode is to avoid the bad stuff.

Humans have a negative bias. We are hardwired to take more notice of negative things than positive. The optimistic, super-positive caveman who wandered out of his cave and pondered the beauty of a rainbow would most likely have been eaten by a tiger. The anxious fella who looked around for danger and was worried about tigers was the one who survived, and he passed his genes on to us. Anxiety and negative bias are there to make us pay attention.

Avoiding pain is our biological first-choice default. Our biology gets the first crack at what we think, feel or do. Avoiding pain is a reflex. Stick your hand on a hot stove and you won't have a debate about whether you should move your hand or not, you just move (quickly) and say, 'Holy shit, that's hot. Let's not do that again' (sea squirt 101). In the brain, the fear centre (your amygdala) is located right next door to the memory centre (the hippocampus). This fortuitous arrangement makes it super-easy to remember the things that scared the shit out of you and not do them again.

Say you try a new system at work and your boss chews you out because it stuffed up the third-quarter figures. Getting criticism from your boss at work will make your inner sea squirt want to move to another part of the sea floor. (Pity you have eaten your brain and are stuck where you are.) Your first shitty draft at what to do might be to quit, yell, avoid your boss or vow never to try anything new that might repeat that feeling. But that's your default reaction (avoid pain). If something feels bad enough, you'll remember it forever and avoid it like a vegan avoids hamburgers.

Our stress hormones – cortisol and adrenaline – drive our 'avoid pain' motivator. These hormones are all about movement and priorities. The fight-or-flight response is there to keep us safe. It gives us the energy to run or box on and prioritises safety.

Cortisol is a prioritising hormone – it turns down the things we don't need to fight or fly, and it upregulates the systems we do need. You don't need your digestive, immune or reproductive systems when you are running away from tigers, so cortisol turns them down. You know that stressed-out friend who has irritable bowel syndrome, is always sick and never gets laid? He's marinating in cortisol, and unless he can work out a way to sort his stress levels, he will be destined for a life of boring food, few friends and lots of trips to the doctor.

In sea squirt mode, we hate pain. The problem is that most good things are on the other side of discomfort, struggle and difficulty. Avoiding challenges and letting your sea squirt's first shitty instinct decide what you feel, think and do is a curious habit.

Seeking pleasure

Just as Thorndike and Skinner discovered, we repeat behaviours that feel good. In sea squirt mode, finding pleasure is about finding what will feel good in the moment.

When it comes to our brain's reward systems, dopamine is the rock star. It's the key to the 'seek pleasure' portion of human motivation. As our 'drive to thrive' hormone, dopamine is responsible for motivating us to move towards things that are pleasurable.

A hungry cavewoman sees an apple tree in the distance; she gets a little squirt of dopamine. Her prehistoric brain starts predicting how good those apples will taste and drops a bit more dopamine into her system, just to keep her interested. When she finally gets the apple and bites into one, her reward system is yelling, 'Yay! Next time you are hungry, remember this place and chow down on some apples'.

Dopamine is crucial for learning and memory; it plays a big part in everything sex, drugs and rock-and-roll. It's the chemical of addiction, but it's also the chemical of focus, concentration and commitment. If we utilise it correctly (big if), dopamine keeps us on track by giving us a little squirt of pleasure when we are on the right path to reach our goals. If we're in sea squirt mode, however, it can make us addicted to whatever gives us pleasure *now*.

Saving energy

As we've learned already, the brain makes up 2 percent of our body weight yet uses 20 percent of our energy. Evolution is a tinkerer, and if we are going to have big, expensive brains, there has to be a benefit, and we need to make them as efficient as possible. Habits are the eco mode to brain function. Ever since we crawled out of the jungle, human brains have been using habits to make things automatic and require less brain energy.

When you get behind the wheel of a car for the first time, you are a bundle of nervous energy. Key here, indicator on, foot on the accelerator, hands at ten and two, check the blind spot… There are a million things to think about, and it's exhausting. However, once you learn how, driving is relaxing and takes very little energy. Once your habits are formed, you don't have to think about them anymore: you are on autopilot.

Once, after a hectic day at work, I drove home to my old house. I'd moved a few weeks prior, and my overloaded brain simply took the route it remembered best. When I drive my wife's car, the windscreen always gets a dry wipe when I'm preparing to turn, as her indicator and wiper levers are on the opposite side to my car.

Habits are all about saving (and freeing up) energy. If we no longer have to think about our basic behaviours, such as walking and choosing what to eat, we can devote more energy to inventing cool stuff. Habits allowed cave dwellers to invent spears and the wheel. The energy saved frees up mental room for intelligent people to invent iPhones, drones and driverless cars.

Dealing with stress uses a lot of brain energy, and a stressful day will turn on your brain's fuel light. The more stress we experience, the more we rely on well-worn habits. Think about your willpower after a particularly stressful day. Say you make a commitment to decrease your sugar intake and have a long-term goal to develop healthier eating habits. Throw in a cranky boss, an unrealistic deadline for your big report, a sick kid and a spouse who decides today is the day to talk about the state of your marriage, and the Toblerone in the cupboard becomes irresistible. Avoiding temptation takes energy; giving in, popping into sea squirt mode and doing something that feels good is way easier. If Toblerone is your habit of choice to quickly feel good, stress will decrease your resistance and have you eating little triangular mountains of chocolatey joy in no time. Feeling good *now* becomes a bigger priority than avoiding diabetes and having pants that fit. I'll talk about stress in much more detail in later chapters.

Old Brain, New Brain

The human brain has developed in layers over thousands of years. There are parts of the brain that all animals have, and parts that are uniquely human. For the purposes of this book (and to indulge my curious habit of wanting to get to the good bits quicker), we are going to simplify the crap out of it. I like to think of it as having an Old Brain and a New Brain.

The Old Brain (which includes the brain stem, limbic system, amygdala and hippocampus) is like your own personal sea squirt running the show. It moves you away from bad and towards good. It is quick, reflexive and is either 'yes' or 'no'. It doesn't care about nuance or shades of grey – everything is black or white. Whenever something happens, your Old Brain gets the first crack at deciding if it's good or bad. It will make you jump out of the way before you've even registered that the bus is going to hit you. It will tell you when the dodgy salesperson is full of shit. Its job is to keep you safe, so it's always on the lookout for things that could hurt you. It has no language centre and doesn't plan for the future, but it is where your emotions (especially fear) and memory are formed.

The New Brain (your prefrontal cortex) is a prediction and planning machine. It's slower, and it weighs up your options and looks for subtleties and patterns that it recognises. The New Brain takes a long time to develop (it's not fully developed until your mid-twenties) because it wants to take into account your environment and whatever it can learn about how the world works. Your New Brain is shaped by your history and past experiences and how you viewed them.

Stanford primatologist Robert Sapolsky argues that the job of your prefrontal cortex is to bias your brain towards **doing the harder thing when the harder thing is the right thing to do**. This may explain why young people, particularly hormone-ravaged teenagers, are slaves to their impulses and find it difficult to concentrate when things get tough: their prefrontal cortexes haven't yet developed and their inner sea squirts are running the show without much help.

The New Brain is the part that helps you get deliberate about what you do. It may take a bit of effort and feel uncomfortable to use initially, but you need the New Brain to get curious if you are ever going to change a habit.

Emotion, memory and action

Can you remember where you were on September 11, 2001? If you're in your thirties or older, what about when Princess Diana was killed? These incidents are imprinted into our collective memories. I can also remember the 1996 Masters Tournament (Greg Norman capitulating), the 1990 AFL Grand Final (still the worst day ever) and the day my daughter was born (these aren't in order of importance, Chloe). I'll never forget the 1979 movie *The Champ*. Nine-year-old me bawled my eyes out when Ricky Schroder's dad died after the boxing match. All of these incidents are indelibly etched into my brain because of the emotions they elicited at the time.

We have a complex network of brain gadgetry that helps us remember. The hippocampus is where memories are formed and it's parked right next door to the amygdala, which is the fear (or emotion) centre. The fear associated with September 11 sent my amygdala into overdrive and made my hippocampus come alive to make sure I remembered as much as I could about that day. It was the morning of my mum's 60th birthday and I was making a video for her on the computer when my sister rang and told me to turn on the news. Seeing the plane fly into the second tower live on TV was horrific. Seeing replays on every channel for the next few weeks only served to strengthen the memory. I don't remember too many of Mum's other birthdays, but I'll never forget her turning 60. (As a 75-year-old, my mum dressed up as a gorilla for her granddaughter's 'jungle' themed birthday party. She's that kind of mum. I remember that party, too.)

Emotion is powerful when it comes to memory-making. It helps us remember the context: where we were and who we were with. The overriding factors that dictate what we remember are how different the incident was to the normal, and how we feel about it.

Eventually, we create a story about the event – and that story becomes the memory. We don't remember the facts of what happened; we remember the story we replay about what happened. And, as we'll find out in later chapters, sometimes those stories can't be trusted (but they can be changed).

Nearly a hundred years ago, Dale Carnegie noticed something that is still true today: 'When dealing with people, remember you are not dealing with creatures of logic, but creatures of emotion'. A lot has changed in the last century, but emotions are still behind a lot of our curious habits. Emotion spurs the Old Brain into action. Imagine your body is a car. The Old Brain is the driver, and it's working hard to dodge other cars, potholes and soft edges (your emotions). It works quickly to respond to every emotion that comes at it. The New Brain is riding shotgun with the map open (remember those?). It doesn't have GPS – it is old-school and likes to see the bigger picture. To get the Old Brain heading in the right direction, it has to give directions on where to go in a way that a sea squirt would understand. The New Brain must also try to explain the Old Brain's snap decisions, often without acknowledging emotions as the driving force – because facing the hard truth of what the emotions are trying to communicate could bring a world of pain.

Have you ever uttered the phrase, 'Why the hell did I do that?' We all have. Most of the time we have made a decision based on emotion and our Old Brain has reacted by reflex, out of habit. The New Brain then comes back online and makes up a story to justify what we just did. A stressed-out road-rager's Old Brain lights up and, before they know it, they are flipping the bird and abusing the poor old lady who inadvertently cut them off. Their Old Brain bypasses any curiosity about emotional cues and surmises that old people shouldn't be driving.

Curious habits incorporate what we feel, think and do, so it's really important to understand the emotions that are sitting under the surface and become aware of what we are thinking in order to have any chance of explaining or changing what we do. As Harvard psychologist Dr Susan David says, by seeing 'emotions as a signpost' and getting curious about what we are feeling and why, we can start to take deliberate action, rather than letting our Old Brains run the show or using logic to explain things after they have happened.

Addiction: when your habits turn on you

Everyone likes Steven. He's a lovely bloke who works hard and always has time for a chat. He is in his mid-forties and is the CEO of a national pharmacy chain. He has the flash car and the house in the posh suburb, and his kids go to an expensive private school.

After completing his pharmacy degree, he started work for a big chain of chemists. He was good at it, and he loved it. His days were spent helping people and he made fantastic connections with customers and staff. He was the sort of chemist who would personally home-deliver medications to sick patients who couldn't get into the store.

Within a few years, Steven married his high-school sweetheart, Kate, and was managing his local branch. The business was going from strength to strength and the two lovebirds bought their first home (and took on the mortgage that went with it). A few more years and a couple of babies later, Steven was offered a state manager position and jumped at the chance. With young kids and a big mortgage, the offer of more money and a company car made the choice easy. It was a promotion, and Steven took it.

The long hours were OK at first, but started to be a problem when the kids hit preschool age. He rarely got home before the kids' bedtime and only really saw them on weekends. Kate started to feel like a single mum. When he was home, Steven started 'relaxing' with a beer, while watching sport on TV or playing video games. Kate and Steven started drifting apart and cracks appeared in their marriage.

Fast-forward 10 years. Steven is CEO, has the corner office and makes a good living. The company is going well, and the board of directors loves his work.

There is only one problem. Steven is miserable. His second marriage is now on the rocks. He still spends most of his time at work, and he's started calling into the pub on the way home for a quick drink to defuse the stress. On the weekend he hits up *Call of Duty* with a bottle of Coke and a bag of chips and doesn't even notice his wife's attempts to rekindle their connection. His kids are now teenagers; they live with Kate and don't really talk to him. He's 30 kilograms (66 pounds) overweight and has just been diagnosed with type 2 diabetes. He's still a nice bloke, but his habits and his priorities have somehow diverged.

Where did it go wrong?

Insidious habits

When I think of addiction, my mind goes to alcohol, heroin and crystal meth. Researching habits, behaviour design and the human reward system, I started to learn about the dark side of habits and what happens when a habit turns into an addiction.

We all have our vices – the sneaky chocolate when no one is looking, the *Fifty Shades of Grey* novel that is shamefully stuck in the bottom drawer under the socks, or the occasional $10 each way on the horses that makes Saturday afternoon a bit more interesting. Small vices aren't addictions – there is a big gap between enjoying a drink on a Friday night and becoming a fall-down drunk who blacks out and falls asleep in a pool of dribble every other night. That said, it's easy for vices to slip into addiction territory when we're not paying attention.

There are two definitions of addiction that I think work well together. The first comes from neuroscientist Andrew Huberman, who defines it as **'a progressive narrowing of things that bring you pleasure'**.

The second is from Dr Judson Brewer, who in his book *The Craving Mind* defines addiction as **'continuing use despite adverse consequences'**.

The obvious addictions that spring to mind – alcohol, drugs (prescription and recreational), tobacco and nicotine, and gambling – can all mess you up when they get out of control. You don't have to explain addiction to the miserable (and unfortunate) drunk, stoned guy, sucking on a ciggie after losing his rent money at the casino.

There is a more subtle type of addiction, though, that can have adverse consequences while narrowing the things that bring you pleasure, such as:

· food
· sex and porn

- work
- coffee (and caffeine)
- shopping
- phones and technology
- video games.

None of these substances or activities are inherently bad in every circumstance. We *need* food, sex is super-fun and phones now live at the bottom level of Maslow's hierarchy of needs (right next to air). Even nicotine has a positive effect on cognitive abilities, fine motor skills, attention and memory (I'm not going to start smoking though!).

The problem is when use becomes compulsive, and it can happen pretty easily. All these examples can become curious habits because they start by firing up the dopamine reward system. This ancient system is your inner sea squirt's 'drive to thrive' or 'want' pathway, designed to keep you focused enough to find food and sex. Dopamine is rewarding for a reason. To paraphrase Dr Judson Brewer, **addiction is like an evolutionary freight train: every abused drug rides on the dopamine express**.

For Steven, the dopamine hits he was getting from his career felt great. He was successful, and that is rewarding. Unfortunately, his lack of work-related boundaries meant his stress bucket was always full, and when he got home, exhaustion sent him searching for dopamine hits to help empty his bucket. Beer, chips and mindless video games became a habit, and the dopamine lollipops they provided gave him instant (albeit short-term) comfort.

The dopamine reward pathway gets the habit started, and before long the habit is ingrained. After that, your brain remembers the complex series of events related to the habit and it doesn't even need the reward pathway anymore. This is when the habit becomes reward invariant – you do it whether it feels good or not. Like curious habits, most addictions are enjoyable until they aren't.

That begs the question: why do it? Once they are addicted, most heroin addicts don't describe using heroin to feel good – they use it to get rid of the terrible feelings they are experiencing. Addiction is a way to alleviate pain.

Addiction specialist Dr Gabor Maté explains that compulsive problems are 'neither a choice nor an inherited disease, but a psychological and physiological response to painful life experiences'. His way of looking at addiction is to understand 'why the pain' rather than 'why the addiction'. He sees addictions as desperate attempts to fix problems: problems of emotional pain, overwhelming stress, lost connections, loss of control, and often a deep discomfort with ourselves and our place in the world.

Often, but not always, the pain is rooted in childhood trauma, and counselling and therapy are required to address the causes. In the past, I thought that people who had hang-ups over childhood trauma just needed to put their big-boy or big-girl pants on and toughen up. To me, blaming your messed-up choices on your childhood was a cop-out and just an excuse for bad behaviour.

It turns out, *I was wrong!* Fortunately, learning about neuroscience, running mental health first-aid courses and talking to clients with trauma has opened my eyes. I learned that in people who have experienced trauma, the painful pathways from childhood have been there for years, and it takes a lot of time and work to build new ones. I have had to check my privilege (thanks Mum and Dad) and have a bit more empathy and compassion for people who have done it tough.

In Steven's case, it turns out that the way he was raised made a big impact on the way he felt about himself. He learned as a child that he could prove his worth by getting all the gold stars. The problem was, that meant his priorities were all skewed towards default rewards like status and money. He loved his life helping customers as a pharmacist, but his default priorities took him away from the connections that brought him joy. Being a workaholic is exhausting, and it can introduce a bunch of other unwanted habits that chip away at connections with family and friends and mess with your mental and physical health.

*

Understanding the evolutionary basis of autopilot and seeing the relationships between emotion, memory and action will help you get curious about your habits. You can use this knowledge to start altering what you feel, think and do – beginning with the next chapter, which covers the basics of habit change.

Chapter 2

Rebundling your habits

'The cure for boredom is curiosity. There is no cure
for curiosity.'
– attributed to Dorothy Parker

The story of Sisyphus is a cautionary tale. In Greek mythology, Sisyphus angered the gods for being too full of himself. He was condemned for all of eternity to the underworld, where he was given the worst possible punishment the gods could hand out. That punishment was to spend every day rolling a boulder up a hill, only to see it roll back down at the end of the day. The gods of ancient Greece were pretty smart and a bit nasty if you pissed them off. They knew what a heart-wrenching, spirit-crushing existence this would be and condemned poor old Sisyphus to spend the rest of eternity in misery.

How many of us are looking at habit change a little bit like Sisyphus? Our 12-hour workdays, tortuous commutes and toxic work cultures would make our Greek friend long for the comfort of his boulder. We are killing ourselves in the gym and miserably living on diets of celery sticks and hummus only to lose three kilograms (seven pounds) and gain four. Are we looking at our goals and pursuing them for the right reasons? Do we want the big house and the flash car because we really like big houses and flash cars, or are we working for these things to impress someone else? Are we filling a void of self-worth with material crap that has little or no value soon after the purchase is made?

Changing habits takes a lot of energy. When you first try to cement a new habit, it not only takes more energy, it delivers worse results. No sea squirt is going to put up with that. Fortunately, we have bigger brains than a sea squirt, though, and by connecting to our longer-term goals – *our* goals, not other people's – we can develop habits that help get us there. It may be hard at first, but once the deliberate habits become our default habits, life gets easier.

Paths in the sand dunes

In the introduction to this book, I mentioned that there are about 86 billion neurons in the average human brain, and each one is connected to thousands of others, creating literally trillions of neural pathways. Some of these pathways are short, some are long; some are weak, and some are strong. It is the activity in these pathways, the neurons talking to each other, that creates all your feelings, thoughts and actions. I like to think of neural pathways as being like paths in a sand dune. Your natural way of walking to the beach is on the most well-worn path. It is possible to walk over the other parts of the dune, but it's more difficult.

Humans are a bit like electricity, or water: we will take the path of least resistance.

Habits are our brains sticking to well-worn paths. We think a certain way because we've always thought a certain way. Our default habits are our well-worn paths that we take automatically without giving it much thought. After a while, these default habits – things we feel, think and do – can take us places we no longer wish to go. That's when they become curious habits.

The good thing is that you can make new paths in the sand dunes. You just have to consciously walk in a different direction to make new well-worn paths – deliberate paths that are in alignment with who you want to be and what you want to feel, think and do.

It takes more effort initially, but getting deliberate about your habits is possible. The great thing about sand dunes (and neural pathways) is that every time you make yourself take that new, deliberate, better path, it becomes a little more worn, until one day soon the deliberate path is the most well-worn default path and you don't even realise that you're taking it. Don't look now, but you have created a new habit – one that you actually want.

There is a major road between my home on the Gold Coast and the city of Brisbane, an hour to the north, called the M1. As you drive to Brisbane, if you look to the right, you can see another two-lane road meandering over the rolling hills parallel to the ten-lane behemoth of the motorway. When I was a kid, the two-lane road was the main road to get to the city.

Building deliberate habits and the neural pathways that accompany them is like building the M1. It's hard, but the effort is worth it when the new habit takes you where you want to go. The curious thing is, the old habit, like the old meandering road, remains as well. It's like remembering words to a song you haven't heard in 20 years, or riding a bike. The pathways of your old habits may not get used anymore, but the old road remains, and you can easily end up travelling along it if you don't pay attention. Being curious and deliberate are the keys to taking the road that helps.

The magic of curiosity

When I was about four years old, I lost a wheel off a red wagon I used to drag around. My uncle Bruce (yep, I'm that Aussie) saw me trying to get the wheel back on and thought this was a job for the shed. He was a grumpy old bugger, but he loved showing me how things worked. The red wagon had white aluminium wheels that stayed on with nothing but an R-clip. Bruce found one in the shed and patiently showed me how to push the clip into the axle and reattach the wheel. I was mesmerised. So simple, but so clever. Even at four years old, being curious felt good.

All kids are naturally curious. They love to know how things work and try new stuff. Pablo Picasso said, 'Every child is an artist. The problem is how to remain an artist once he grows up'. The problem is that our curiosity is shut down as we get older.

In his book *Think Again*, Wharton business school professor Adam Grant says it's important to unlearn the things you think you know. We all have a database of pain inside our heads – we remember the time we forgot our line in the school play; we remember the girlfriend who left because we showed vulnerability. As adults, our databases are full, and we have developed habit loops with neural pathways supporting them. Our sea squirt decisions become our identity, and the habits we develop can kill curiosity.

Having a brain that is super-flexible and constantly making new connections makes learning easier for kids. As adults, we deal with life by relying on default ways of thinking and, as Grant explains, it's often the unlearning that takes all the effort.

Let's go back to our three motivators – avoid pain, seek pleasure and save energy. Being wrong can fire up habits related to the dominant 'avoid pain' motivator. Being wrong can be embarrassing and decrease your confidence. No one wants that, so we avoid being wrong.

Remember, from an evolutionary standpoint, avoiding pain is the big one – the default. Fail to avoid the tiger and you don't get to contribute to evolution. If blame and shame are attached to being wrong, we will be even more likely to avoid doing that again.

To remain curious, we have to throw in 'the joy of being wrong' and look at new information as a **thought upgrade**. I think of being wrong like a cold shower for the mind: it may not feel great in the moment, but it's good for me; and if I learn to like it, I can drop unwanted curious habits more easily and upgrade to a way of thinking that helps. It's often tempting to dig your heels in and fight for your old way of thinking when new information contradicts the old. Studies show that the longer we have had a certain way of thinking and the more invested we are in it, the harder it is to change those habits.

Dave Mustaine was really invested in his curious habit of being angry. It bought him success and accolades, along with a lot of pain, addiction and grief. To survive in the world, he had to rethink everything he thought he knew. Eventually, the angry, hard-arse rock star changed. He got sober; he found God. He became fuelled by curiosity about what he was getting out of his old habits. He still wrote big, eardrum-bursting songs that his fans loved, but he learned to do it from a place of gratitude, acceptance and purpose.

Default habit loops

In chapter 1, I introduced Thorndike's concept of the habit loop. A whole bunch of things we do follow habit loops. Smell cookies (trigger), eat cookies (behaviour) and get a tasty sugary hit (reward). Boom, that tasted great, let's do that again. The more we perform a certain habit loop, the easier it becomes and the more we start to repeat it automatically.

Most books about habits talk about some variation of trigger, behaviour and reward as the habit loop. The habit loop we are going to get curious about is slightly different. I describe the habit loop as shown in Figure 2.1, overleaf.

Figure 2.1: Cue, action, result

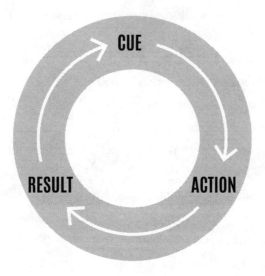

Cues get the habit started; action is what you do next; and the result is what you get out of it. To alter your habits, you need to get curious about each of these points, particularly the result.

A good surprise results in a dopamine spike that makes you want to repeat the action. There is a new Vietnamese restaurant at the end of my street, and the first time I went there I ordered spring rolls. These spring rolls were the bomb! Inside was a creamy, spicy Thai red chicken curry that was not what I expected. It was a surprise taste sensation, and my brain got a massive surge of dopamine: 'Remember where you got these little cylindrical parcels of joy – I want to do that again'. If my wife and I are trying to choose somewhere for dinner, the Vietnamese place always gets the nod from me. I want those red curry spring rolls again.

Forming habits is all about the reward. We know that emotion drives memory. We remember the bad things and avoid them. Memories of pleasant things we have liked in the past drive our wants and cravings: 'That was nice, let's do that again' (think sex, chocolate, love, winning, cold beer and red curry spring rolls). Our brains have a database of experience from the past to rate things against each other. Do you prefer ice cream or cauliflower? Most people don't take long to decide with a choice like that: only the extremely lactose intolerant vegans would pick cauliflower in that pair. Our brains are good at predicting rewards, and when they get it wrong, it's memorable.

Cues, not triggers

After you pull the trigger on a gun, you have no control over where the bullet is going to go. We use the word 'trigger' when we're describing a lot of things, particularly around anxiety, arguments and aggression. It's a word that sounds ominous while taking away our sense of control, choice and autonomy. If something 'triggers' a behaviour, we have no control over what we do and end up on autopilot.

The word 'cue', on the other hand, leaves space for curiosity.

When we get curious about what we feel, think and do, we can start to make choices that rise above sea squirt mode. The newest, most evolved part of our brain is the prefrontal cortex – it's the planning and prediction centre, and curiosity is impossible without it. Curiosity gives us a view of the bigger picture and helps us make choices in line with our long-term goals rather than the instant gratification of sea squirt mode. If we can get curious about how we feel and think – our cues – we have more control over what we do.

When I run Stress RESET workshops with my clients, I spend a lot of time talking about triggers – particularly with regard to anxiety. I ask everyone to get curious about the first symptoms they experience when they begin to feel stressed and anxious. The answers vary, but there is always someone with knots in the stomach; others experience an elevated heart rate or tightness in the chest. One curiously anxious fella discovered that he knew he was feeling anxious when he started 'sweating out of his head'.

Recognising your initial physical feeling when stress and anxiety pop up is an essential first step to self-awareness. If you let the physical feelings trigger your response without curiosity intervening, you can end up in what I call an 'Old-Brain Shitstorm'. This is when the fight-or-flight system feeds itself and amplifies the problem. Knots in your stomach trigger a quickening heart rate, causing the fear centre (your amygdala) to light up like a Christmas tree while the logical, smart part of your brain goes offline, along with any hope of a deliberate response. Curious, huh!

By changing your thinking from 'triggers for anxiety' to 'cues to get curious', you give yourself more space to look at your options and choose the habit loop that helps. When you do this, you step out of your default loop and into your new deliberate loop. If you go around the deliberate loop enough times, you lay down new neural pathways and eventually, your new deliberate loop becomes the default. You stop walking along the old default path and let the grass start to grow over it, making it less obvious. Once this happens, you develop what I like to call 'mindless control'. You are no longer pushing Sisyphus's habit boulder uphill; you have changed a curious habit and created a new default that actually helps.

What have you done for me lately?

Anxiety, addiction and habits expert Dr Judson Brewer helps people decrease anxiety, stop smoking and improve their eating by using mindfulness, understanding reward-based learning and mapping habit loops. His *Craving to Quit!* app is starting to change the way people look at giving up smoking. By helping people get curious about why they smoke and what their triggers for smoking are,

Dr Jud helps people identify the things that start them craving a cigarette – in other words, he gets people to map out all their cues. One app user discovered that he smoked to get rid of the bitter taste of coffee. Another worked out that she smoked whenever she was on the phone.

It sounds really easy to say 'Stop drinking coffee' or 'Grab a glass of water when you get a phone call', but Dr Jud's research shows that this 'swapping one loop for another' strategy has limited success. You need another step.

While identifying your cues is helpful, the secret sauce of change is curiosity – namely, 'What am I getting out of this?' Dr Jud added a step that made a huge difference, and that step is disenchantment. By becoming disenchanted with the results your action delivers, you are more likely to successfully reroute your habit loops.

Remember, curious habits are things you feel, think or do that are no longer helping. It's easy to get disenchanted with something like smoking. One *Craving to Quit!* user described cigarettes as 'smelling like stinky cheese and tasting like chemicals, YUCK!' It's easy to get disenchanted with that. Unwanted thoughts and feelings are a bit more difficult to recognise and change (more on that later).

When the result we expect from an action is different from the result we actually get, this is what psychologists call 'reward prediction error'. With awareness and curiosity, we can spark the desire to change; but if we don't recognise that a habit sucks (and get disenchanted), we have no cue to get curious and change it.

The red curry spring rolls I talked about earlier had a positive reward prediction error – they were way better than I expected, and that helped change my restaurant habits.

Negative reward prediction errors can also change our habits, but they need awareness and disenchantment to do the heavy lifting. This can be difficult to do when a habit is deeply ingrained.

David Neal and habits guru Wendy Wood at the University of Southern California recruited movie-goers at a local cinema to rate a collection of short films. The participants were told their opinions about the films were important, and to say thank you for participating they'd be given *free* popcorn. In another case of scientific switchery, half the participants were given fresh, buttery popcorn and the other half were given stale popcorn that had been stored in a plastic bag and left to fester for seven days. The rubbery popcorn was like salty bits of kitchen sponge and several participants described it as 'disgusting', but lots of people still ate it. The researchers looked at the data and measured how much fresh and stale popcorn was eaten. What they found tells us a lot about habits, autopilot and rewards.

People who always had popcorn at the movies ate just as much stale popcorn as they did the fresh, buttery stuff. If they had a habit of eating popcorn at the cinema, it didn't matter if the popcorn was good or not – they ate it anyway. When they were asked, 'How was the popcorn?', these people answered that it was gross, but they ate it anyway.

The people who didn't habitually have popcorn at the movies ate the good stuff but left the feral stale stuff alone. Without an established popcorn habit, people noticed the negative reward prediction error and were able to resist the free 'treat'.

Once a habit is established, we continue to do it even if it no longer works. Ingrained habits become 'reward invariant' – you don't even need rewards like tasty, buttery crunch to eat popcorn if eating popcorn at the movies is your default.

The researchers followed up with another experiment that offered popcorn to people in the research lab who were invited in to assess the quality of some music videos. In this setting, even the biggest popcorn fans ditched the soggy stale stuff and only ate the fresh popcorn. By changing the environment, the researchers changed the cues and, in doing so, turned off the autopilot and weakened the strength of the habit. Without autopilot, awareness increased, and the participants began to notice the rewards (or lack of them) that they were getting from the bad popcorn. A lot of habits are context-dependent – the time and place provide cues and get the habit loop started, and keep it going.

I'm a sucker for a good meat pie. When I was a kid, my dad would get me one every time we went to the footy. Meat and gravy, surrounded by pastry and drowned in sauce – you beauty! Throw in some great memories of playing footy and hanging with my dad, and pies became something with a high reward value. For me, pies ticked all the caveman reward boxes: they provided safety, great taste, lots of calories and a sprinkle of nostalgia, making them the perfect recipe for a habit worth repeating.

The only problem is, they don't love me. Pies give me serious heartburn and make my stomach feel terrible. They are great going in, but I pay for it later (with a sore chest and tighter pants). The reward prediction (from really great memories) is that the pie will taste great and stop me from feeling hungry. The actual result is regret and a sore stomach.

Getting curious, noticing the result and becoming disenchanted with the difference between the expected reward and the actual result is the key to habit change. You have to notice when there is a difference between the predicted reward and the actual reward if you are ever going to change (see Figure 2.2, overleaf).

With a habit like smoking or eating a heartburn-inducing pie, it's easy to see where the action took a turn for the worse. Some other curious habits, particularly around anxiety, feelings and thinking, are a bit more subtle. We'll look at those more closely in the later parts of this book.

Figure 2.2: Expected reward versus actual result

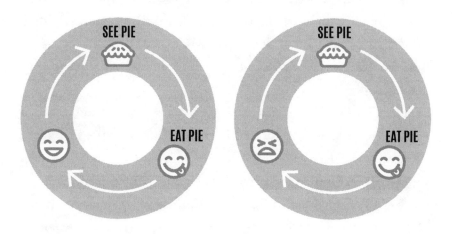

Deliberate 10-year-old pie loop   Default 50-year-old pie loop

The infinite loop and tidal habits

When most people think of habits, diet and exercise are usually top of mind: 'If I can improve my diet, I'll lose 5.4 kilograms (12 pounds) and everything will be good'. The problem is, no habit operates in a vacuum. Habits are like a bowl of spaghetti: they are intertwined and influence each other.

There are five big factors that affect our health and wellness, and each one has an influence on the other four:

1. food
2. mood
3. move (exercise)
4. snooze
5. stress (this comes in at the crossroads of the other four).

It looks a bit like Figure 2.3.

Figure 2.3: The infinite loop of health

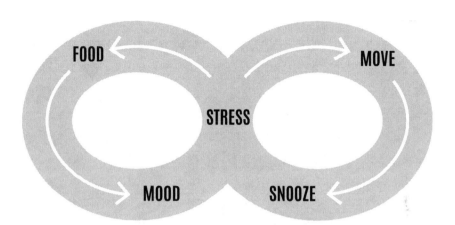

If something is off with our food, mood, sleep or exercise, this can quickly derail the others.

We all have a stress bucket: a finite quantity of things that we can deal with and still function at our best. I recently had shoulder surgery (old man injury) and the combination of pain, difficulty sleeping and inability to exercise made me cranky, stressed and looking for anything that would make me feel good. I couldn't concentrate, so reading was out. I couldn't move, so exercise was out. The only thing that would lift my mood was chocolate, and even that was fleeting, as guilt and the imminent expansion of my waistline threw another rock in my stress bucket.

Dr Harry Weisinger operates a medical practice called My Performance Doctor, in which he uses health monitoring, diet, supplements, behaviour change and exercise to help athletes (and people like me) get their health on point so they can perform at their best. Dr Harry believes we can only really have two big priorities for change at any one time. Health and study, for example. Or relationships and fitness. Or diet and family. He gets analogue and describes it like a dual tape deck: if you want to put a new tape in, you have to take one out. And you can only listen to one of the two tapes on your tape deck at a time.

I put Dr Harry's theory to cognitive neuroscientist Dr Mick Zeljko (the co-author of my first book, *Stress Teflon*), and he agreed. Mick explained that attention is like a spotlight, and you need a lot of cognitive control (brain effort) to get a new habit to stick. You need to shine the spotlight onto the systems involved in the new habit to effect change. Mick's suggestion is to find and concentrate on what he calls a 'tidal habit'.

As the old adage goes: **a rising tide lifts all boats**.

When I shared my infinite loop of health habits with Mick, he asked me a simple question: 'Which one of those things, if you get it right, will lift all the others?' They all affect each other, but for most people, one will be the most effective entry point.

I thought about the five things on the loop and realised that my tidal habit was exercise. I do at least an hour of exercise every morning. My usual routine is to get up between 4 a.m. and 5 a.m., write for an hour, and then get on my exercise bike and read on my Kindle while I pedal and sweat like a madman. As long as I do this exercise, my food, mood and snooze stay on track and I'm able to handle whatever stress comes my way.

So, it made sense that when the shoulder surgery hijacked my exercise routine, the tide started dropping on all points of my infinite loop. Something had to change.

I decided to move the exercise bike into the middle of my bench-press rack so I could ride sitting upright (holding the weights bar) and not damage my shoulder by leaning over. I added a music stand to hold my Kindle, and all of a sudden I had my tidal habit back: I could exercise again. My mood improved, there was no need for chocolate because I wasn't kicking stones anymore, and a few strategically placed pillows got me back into the land of zzz. The one habit of exercise had a massive influence on all the others and 'lifted all boats'.

When it comes to the infinite loop, you can't overestimate the importance of sleep. Sleep is the brain's way of cleaning itself and washing away the waste. A good night's sleep elevates your mood and increases your willpower. If the benefits of sleep were available in a pill, Big Pharma would make a fortune. It really is a curious habit to sacrifice snooze for anything less important.

There is a term in psychology called 'revenge sleep procrastination' that describes the decision to sacrifice sleep for leisure time. Late-night Netflix bingeing with a family block of chocolate or infinitely scrolling TikTok are not going to help any of the categories on your infinite loop. Revenge sleep procrastination is about gaining some autonomy (and joy) when your daily schedule is lacking in free time or fun. For people in high-stress jobs that take up the bulk of their day, revenge sleep procrastination is a way to find a few hours of instant gratification, even though it results in insufficient sleep that drags the rest of the infinite loop down.

To stop revenge sleep procrastination, I learned an easy reframe: **start your day the night before**.

By starting my day eight hours before I want to get up, I am less likely to watch that extra episode of *Modern Family* and go to bed on time. I really enjoy my early-morning serenity and exercise; no way would I swap that for a late-night sitcom.

Getting curious and finding *your* tidal habit is worth doing. Maybe it's sleep; maybe it's food. Being overwhelmed and stressed can take the tide out and drop all the others. Tides go both ways, and knowing what lowers all your boats is just as helpful. Getting curious will help you find your tidal habits; do that and everything improves.

Let's get curious

- Map out some default habit loops and see how they are serving you.
- What are the triggers, and how can you use them as cues to get curious?
- What is your tidal habit?

Chapter 3

Making deliberate your default

'Insanity is doing the same thing over and over
and expecting different results.'
– Albert Einstein

Christie was living in her car. Six months' pregnant and with her one-year-old son Oscar in the baby seat behind her, Christie had driven her tiny vehicle 1200 kilometres from the country Victorian town of Shepparton to the Gold Coast. Sharing a three-door Hyundai with a toddler was never going to be a long-term strategy, though. Something had to change.

In her own words, Christie's life was a 'shitstorm'. She'd been living in a town ravaged by the ice epidemic; all her friends used the drug and lots of them were addicts. She had managed to get 'off the gear' and was trying her best to make a life for herself and little Oscar. An offer from her cousin to come and live on the Gold Coast was just the fresh start her growing family needed. The opportunity to escape her abusive boyfriend and a town full of triggers to use drugs was too good to refuse.

She arrived at her cousin's flat late on a Friday afternoon, anxious to wash the 1200 kilometres of road grime off herself and Oscar. Tired and broke, she was upbeat about her new start – only to have her bubble burst by the news that her cousin had passed away two days earlier. She wasn't welcome in the flat, and she knew nobody on the Gold Coast. Her shit sandwich of a life had just got a bit worse.

I met Christie a few days later at a charity kitchen I volunteered at on Tuesday mornings. We had a chat over breakfast, and I was amazed by her bravery and how determined she was to stay off drugs. She was going to give her son a life and a mum to be proud of. She was from Scotland, and she had a stereotypically Scottish stoic toughness about her. To Christie, a life without drugs was something she was willing to work for, and if it meant being lonely and sleeping in her car, that's what she was going to do.

Christie's outlook is something we can all learn from.

In chapter 1 we talked about the curious habit of addiction – of continuing to do something despite severe adverse consequences. Christie had a drug habit that was ruining her life. It was orders of magnitude worse than eating stale popcorn or getting heartburn from a pie, but the basis of change was the same. To change, Christie needed to step out of her old default habit loops and build some new habits that helped.

As we learned from the popcorn experiment in chapter 2, changing the environment changes the habit cues. This can give us space to get curious and see our habits for what they really are – to let in our disenchantment with the results we're getting. Switching the movie theatre for a lab gave people the space to become aware that they weren't enjoying the stale snacks. To Christie, Shepparton was full of people and places that reminded her of drugs. Moving to a new town was a *reset* that helped her swap out her default habit loops for new, deliberate ones that helped.

Wharton business school professor and behaviour change expert Katy Milkman is an economist who studies behaviour change in business. She coined the term 'fresh start effect'. New Year's Day, milestone birthdays, new months and Mondays are all examples of times to make a fresh start. New Year's resolutions get a bad rap – a 2007 survey found that one-third of all New Year's resolutions are abandoned by 1 February. Milkman pushes back on the idea that resolutions are ineffective, though. Her results show that 20 percent of the goals set in January succeed.

In her book *How to Change*, Milkman outlines some strategies that can improve the odds. She says our problem is that 'we search for solutions that will deliver the quick knockout victory and tend to ignore the specific nature of our adversary'. According to Katy, we must all customise our strategy by first understanding where we go astray. As Sun Tzu said, 'Know thy enemy'. By understanding our weak spots, we can avoid making the same mistakes over and over again.

Motivation and sales author Dan Pink introduced the idea of a pre-mortem. We all know about post-mortems – the coroner gives the dead dude a thorough going-over and works out the cause of death. A pre-mortem looks at the possible ways things can go wrong and helps you put systems in place to avoid the bad stuff happening. Without knowing it, Christie had done a pre-mortem of her addictions, and her way of mitigating the danger was to move and get a fresh start.

A 1994 study of people wanting to make meaningful life changes found that big changes were helped along by people moving house. Thirty-six percent of people made substantial life changes following a change of location. This is the hope that Christie was clinging to. Changing her environment and the triggers that went along with it might be just what her little family needed. With the help of some government and charitable organisations, we managed to find Christie and Oscar some accommodation and hopefully a fresh start.

Action gives you answers

Changing your environment, along with the cues and triggers that go with it, is a great place to start when you are looking to get curious about habits. Removing triggers that don't help and planting cues that do can certainly help us build new habit loops – but no change is possible without *action*! To switch from default to deliberate habit loops, we need to *do* something different.

In February 2014, a union strike brought the London Underground system to a halt. Millions of commuters had to find an alternative way to get to work. For 48 hours, the transport system in the British capital was in chaos.

Commuters are habitual beasts and tend to take the same routes on the same trains every day. The strike threw a spanner in the works, and commuters had to get creative and find other ways to get to work.

Economists from Cambridge and Oxford universities measured people's movements before, during and after the strike and found something remarkable. You would assume that people would go back to their old habits as soon as the trains were running again, and most did – but not all.

Following the strike and the resumption of Tube services, 1 in 20 (5 percent) of people chose to stick with their new-found mode of transport. The disruption in services had made them change their long-held habits, and thousands of people discovered a new, *better* way to get to work.

Action gave the commuters answers. Being forced to try something new gave Tube users a look at another option, and then curiosity helped weigh the options. When a commuter caught a bus or rode their pushbike, their brain did a quick calculation to see which option was better.

Figure 3.1: Moving from default loop to deliberate loop

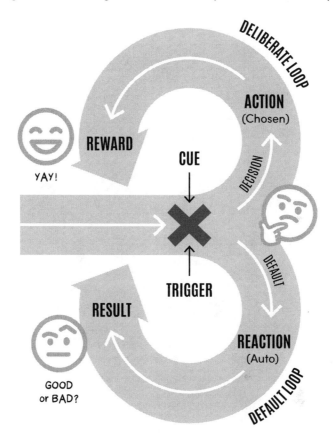

Habits SWAP

The habits SWAP is a simple way to swap out your default habit loops for new, deliberate habit loops that serve you. It works on the basis that, if we get curious, we can see the other options available to us. When you get good at the habits SWAP, you can swap chocolate for an apple, aggression for acceptance and anxiety for excitement. Noticing the cues, getting curious and disenchanted, and choosing the loop that helps is a stress-free way to change habits.

There are four pieces to the SWAP puzzle. You need to:

1. be **SELECTIVE**
2. use **WILLPOWER** wisely
3. cultivate **AWARENESS**
4. be **PERSISTENT**.

Figure 3.2: The habits SWAP

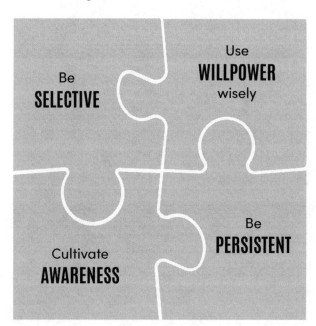

Be selective

To paraphrase Roman philosopher Seneca, if you don't know what port you are heading for, no wind is favourable.

Selecting the habit that is no longer helping is a critical step in changing your curious habits. The first step to solving any problem is acknowledging that there is one. Once you feel disenchantment with the old habit, you can then select a new one to replace it.

In *Atomic Habits*, James Clear said the new, replacement habit must be 'obvious, attractive, easy and satisfying'. If the new habit ticks all of these boxes, it should be a good habit to SWAP for the curious one that has run its race.

In chapter 2 we talked about cues, and these can be used in a deliberate way to select and set up a new habit. My client Adam is a super-busy real estate agent who is often attached to his phone. He would have a long day and was often still taking calls into the evening when he got home. His family life was suffering from their lack of quality time, and it was causing strain for his wife and kids. Adam didn't realise quite how bad things were until 'Bring Dad to school day' at his daughter's school. His daughter's teacher asked, 'What's your dad's favourite thing to do?' The answer: 'Talk on the phone'. It hit poor Adam in the guts, and he realised he needed to change his phone habits.

We talked about it in a coaching session, and he decided to select a new habit of turning his phone off on his way home from work. To cue him to do this, we chose a particular hill about five minutes from his home that would signal him to select 'Dad mode'. He would finish the call he was on and divert his phone to a message that said, 'I am in dad mode at the moment and will call you in the morning'. He then had five minutes to decompress and select the 'state' he wanted to arrive home in.

Defining a cue kicked off the new habit that he had selected, and defining how he wanted to turn up created an action and result that he wanted. His curious habit of being distracted (by the phone) and cranky at home was no longer helping him. He selected a new habit that would allow him to be present, attentive and happy when he got home. By selecting a new habit – complete with cue, action and a (desirable) result – he turned up in the right state to be the dad and husband he wanted to be. Turning his phone off at the top of the hill ticked all of James Clear's boxes: it was 'obvious, attractive, easy and satisfying', particularly when he saw how happy his family was to have him 100 percent present at home.

Part of being selective about your new habit is being clear about what Dr Jud calls your 'bigger, better offer'. If you are going to go to the effort of changing a habit, being selective and choosing a bigger, better offer gives you motivation to stick to that goal even when other obvious short-term goals try to tempt you off course. Selecting a bigger, better offer boosted Adam's motivation to change.

Use willpower wisely

If emotion and the Old Brain drive action, willpower relies on the New Brain to push against the default.

Dr Benjamin Hardy, author of *Willpower Doesn't Work*, and Kelly McGonigal, author of *The Willpower Instinct*, explain in their books why willpower works – until it doesn't. Both agree that willpower is like a muscle: the more you use it, the stronger it gets; but overload it and the muscle tires and weakens. Think of it like doing push-ups: the more push-ups you do, the more you can do. If you try (without training) to do 100 push-ups without a break, though, you will most likely fall on your face. As with your muscles, if you try to rely on willpower too much (especially without any training), your attempt at habit change will eventually fail.

McGonigal describes willpower in this way: **'Willpower is about harnessing the three powers of I will, I won't and I want to help you achieve your goals'**.

For example, I *will* exercise every day, I *won't* live on a diet of burgers and chocolate, and I *want* to be fit and healthy.

The thing about willpower is that it takes effort from the New Brain – in other words, it takes cognitive control.

Stanford researcher Robert Sapolsky, whom we met in chapter 1, says that your New Brain's job is to bias your brain toward doing the harder thing when the harder thing is the right thing to do. It's easy to procrastinate on the monster assignment that's due next week, but the New Brain steps in to say, 'I *will* get started today, even if watching Netflix is easier'. It's easy to say 'yes' to a pint of chocolate-chip Häagen-Dazs. Your emotional Old Brain loves chocolate chips, but your New Brain is biased towards the harder thing. It pipes in and says, 'I *won't* have ice cream today' because it remembers your longer-term goals – 'I *want* to be healthy' – and engages your willpower muscle, enabling you to choose an apple instead.

This sounds like a good system, right? Unfortunately, like a muscle, it works until it doesn't. Stress, tiredness, decision fatigue (too many choices) and constant cravings can weaken the New Brain's ability to do the job of making you do the harder thing when the harder thing is the right thing to do. When the New Brain goes offline, the willpower muscle fails, and we give in to whatever the easy option is. As Dr Benjamin Hardy says, 'Your willpower is basically your energy stores. Once you run out, you're out.'

Dr Hardy proposes that we need to set up our environment to make the thing we want to do the thing that's easy to do. By doing this, we maintain our energy reserves to use willpower when we need it the most.

My friend Mark says he only uses **15 seconds of willpower** at a time. He explained that he's a chocoholic and would always buy a Mars bar every time he was at the petrol station or at the shop to get milk. Wanting to change this habit, he developed his '15 seconds of willpower' tool. While paying for petrol and surrounded by impulse-purchase chocolate (cue), he would say to himself, 'I've got 15 seconds of willpower in me' (action: don't buy chocolate) and have a little smile to himself as he walked outside sans chocolate and congratulated himself for outsmarting the chocolate devils (great result). The '15 seconds of willpower' tool is great because it doesn't use up too much energy, and it makes the 'I won't' choice easier.

It's also important to be aware of your environment when it comes to willpower. Dr Hardy says, 'It takes a lot of willpower to remain positive in a negative environment'. We will get curious about changing our environment later in the book.

Choose your willpower battles wisely. Give your New Brain what it needs to help you stay in your deliberate habit loops.

Cultivate awareness

You can't get curious about a habit SWAP without awareness. The better your awareness, the better your choices. As you make better choices, you will see better results.

There are a few things you need to be especially aware of, because without them, you are walking around blindfolded trying to hit a piñata that's in another room.

The first is your physical feelings – what's going on in your body. Scientists call this 'introspection', and it is all about being conscious of your body's feelings. If you're not aware of your bodily sensations, it's easy to miss cues to get curious. Butterflies in your stomach could indicate nervousness, fear or perhaps hunger. Remember, the caveman who never felt anxious got eaten by tigers and didn't pass on his DNA to us. Feelings are evolutionary, and their job is to alert us to possible danger. If you don't consciously become aware of them, they can start to feel like your normal operating mode. It's like living near an airport – after a while, you don't even hear the planes. Without awareness of your body's cues, you don't think to look for other options and you stick to your default habits.

The second important thing to be aware of is the potential pitfalls that could stop your new habit loop from being successful.

Again, doing a pre-mortem can help: looking at all the possible things that could get in the way of the new habit, so you can put plans in place to mitigate the negative effects. If you know that talking politics with your drunk Uncle Phil will end in an argument and spoil Christmas, a pre-mortem would involve creating a response to have ready to avoid the drama and steer the conversation away from politics. Being aware of possible problems lets you be deliberate about solving them before they eventuate.

Lastly, it's important to be aware of the things you can't change. My body has a lot of weird-arse idiosyncrasies. I'm a bit pigeon-toed, have big hips, a muscle missing in my chest and the world's worst jawline (no chin). I have round shoulders, no hair (it's shaved but the front line is marching back like the French cavalry) and a muscle missing in my left eye which gives me double vision when I look to the right (I couldn't read until grade 9). My wife, Karen, rattled these all off one day and told me, 'God made you just so he could see what you'd look like'. He didn't make another one, but she loves me anyway.

I'd love to look like Chris Hemsworth, but even with my mixed bag of physical peculiarities, it's still good being me. If I spent all my time trying to change what I can't, I'd have no time left to get curious about habits. I've accepted what I know I can't change to give me energy to work on what I can. Psychotherapist and writer Nathaniel Branden said it best: '**The first step toward change is awareness. The second step is acceptance**'.

Be persistent

Are you *interested* in change, or *committed*? I guess that's where perseverance comes in. How much do you want it? If you are committed to change, persistence is the secret sauce.

All great heroes persevere through tough times. When I think of perseverance, Sir Edmund Hillary, Ernest Shackleton, Nelson

Mandela and Ruth Bader Ginsberg (the second female to sit on the US Supreme Court) come to mind. The ability to keep going despite enormous setbacks defines films like *Star Wars*, *The Wizard of Oz* and even *Finding Nemo*. We love a hero story, even when it is about a little orange-and-white fish.

However, enjoying stories about perseverance and finding perseverance within ourselves are two different beasts. In her book *Grit*, psychologist and MacArthur 'Genius' Fellow Angela Duckworth championed the notion that GRIT (yes, it should be all capitals!) is a key ingredient to success. She says: 'As much as talent counts, effort counts twice'. (Can't you imagine that on an inspirational '90s poster with a cat hangin' in there?) Like awareness and willpower, without perseverance, nothing changes.

Habit change can be uncomfortable, and we need a liberal slice of perseverance and GRIT – balanced with curiosity, clarity and an open mind – to keep going. There is a great quote by Abraham Lincoln that goes, 'Be sure to put your feet in the right place, then stand firm'. His wisdom and persistence ended slavery and it can stop you being a slave to dodgy habits.

Curious about your cues

Stanford behaviour change professor B.J. Fogg has been called the 'millionaire maker'. A bunch of Silicon Valley's bigwigs have attended his Persuasive Technology Lab, and his book *Tiny Habits* is a *New York Times* bestseller. Professor Fogg is a modern-day B.F. Skinner.

We've looked at the structure of how habit loops work (cue, action, result) and how reward prediction affects what we do. Fogg's tiny habits model helps take the stress out of cementing your new deliberate habit loops.

Step one is to 'anchor' your new habit to something you already do. Say you want to remember to take a multivitamin. The cue you might anchor that to is brushing your teeth: 'When I put my toothbrush down, I take my pills'. Psychologists call this 'habit stacking', and it's a good way to get a new habit started.

Step two is to make the new habit easy. If you want to start a meditation habit, start with 60 seconds of belly breathing. If you want to do more, you can, but start easy.

Step three – and this is a game-changer for me – is to celebrate doing the new habit. Every time I finish an exercise routine, I celebrate by congratulating myself. Fogg calls this 'SUNSHINE', and adding it to the end of the habit loop will help add positive emotion to the action and make you want to repeat it.

Before getting curious about stress and habits, I had a curious habit of eating chocolate-chip cookies and drinking Pepsi Max when my stress bucket got full. A busy day at work, coupled with not taking a break (another curious habit), would result in a stressful feeling of discomfort, tension and agitation. My default habit loop was cookies with a Pepsi chaser.

Eating fires up your body's 'rest and digest' (parasympathetic) system and has a calming effect for a few minutes. I wanted to feel calmer and less agitated. Sea squirt mode kicked in, and without thinking, I was moving away from stress and towards the pleasures of sugar and caffeine (both of which are like throwing petrol on an anxiety fire to try and put out the flames, but more on that later). What I wanted was calm; what I was getting was bigger pants and a sugar- and caffeine-fuelled vicious circle of stress and anxiety. How else could I empty my stress bucket and decrease the agitation?

A friend had told me about the benefits she had gotten from meditation, and I had scoffed. No way could I meditate. I tried a guided meditation on YouTube a few times. Some hippy with a stoned 'calming' voice was trying to get me to 'imagine a peaceful lake'. Before I knew it, there was a golf course on the shore of the lake and I was riding on a jet ski to mind-surf a left-hand point break that had magically appeared. I was no good at meditation. She suggested I try doing two minutes of 'belly breathing' whenever I felt a bit agitated. I could do two minutes.

The next time I got that overwhelmed feeling, I took her advice and lay down on the floor in my office and concentrated on breathing into my stomach. It was easier than I thought. Whenever my mind wandered, I bought it back to breathing, and the two minutes flew by. When I stood up after that first belly breathing attempt, it felt amazing. The tense, agitated feeling was gone, and I felt calm, refreshed and ready to take on the rest of my day. I made a mental note to do that again. SUNSHINE!

The cue was feeling agitated, and when I felt the familiar craving to devour cookies and Pepsi, I made a mental note to pause and consciously look at my options. My old, default loop was cookies and Pepsi. My new deliberate habit was to meditate – and, like Fogg recommends, I made the habit easy by choosing to do two minutes of belly breathing rather than attempting a 60-minute visualisation meditation. The result I was after was to feel refreshed and calmer. The new habit did that without the guilt of eating crap food. I added some SUNSHINE to my habit loop and within a few weeks, I had swapped the default action of junk food for the deliberate action of belly breathing. Noticing the good feeling reinforced the new loop, and eventually it became my go-to of choice when I was overloaded and wanted to feel better.

No commuters wanted the 2014 Tube strike, but thousands of them benefited from it. I didn't want to do meditation, I just wanted to reduce the feelings of overwhelm and stress. Trying something new opened up options, and getting curious about the results helped change the default into a deliberate habit that eventually will become the new default.

Not all your attempts at change will work. Catching the bus or meditating may suck for you, but trying something new and getting curious about the results is the best way to change what you do. **Action gives you answers.**

Let's get curious

Now that we know a bit more about how habits form and how to change them, let's get curious with a few questions:

- What are some stories you are telling yourself that aren't helping?
- What have you been doing for a long time that is no longer serving you?
- What triggers can you turn into cues to get curious?
- Where can you use 15 seconds of willpower?
- When was the last time you were wrong and had a 'thought upgrade'?
- What is your desired result, and what options have you got to get there?

PART II

THE CURIOUS HABITS

So, we now understand why we have habits, how they form, and what default and deliberate habit loops are. We know about neural pathways and Old and New Brains. Triggers have turned into **cues to get curious**, and we have an idea of what's needed to SWAP from default to deliberate loops. It's time to look at some curious habits and what you can do to change them.

Chapter 4

Staying comfortable

'Comfort zones – If you're in one too long, that becomes your norm. Get comfortable being uncomfortable.'
– David Goggins

David Goggins has transformed his life and his health by ignoring his inner sea squirt, embracing discomfort and finding joy in pushing the physical and mental limits of what a crazy person can do.

Part masochist, part freak and 100 percent warrior, he has a view that, 'Suffering is a test. That's all it is. Suffering is the true test of life'.

His book *Can't Hurt Me* is a bestseller that has shown millions of people the joy to be gained from getting curious about what's possible, and getting comfortable with discomfort.

From humble beginnings, Goggins did it tough. (He calls himself Goggins. Luke loves it when people refer to themselves in the third person.)

His abusive father owned a rollerskating rink and the whole family was expected to work there every night, often until after midnight. The combination of school and work, and having to watch his father beat his mother (and occasionally him) with a belt, made young David a nervous wreck. Deprived of sleep, he often drifted off in class and was threatened with expulsion or removal to a special school. Eventually, when David was nine years old, he and his mother escaped and moved to another town and away from the beatings.

Virtually illiterate, David cheated his way through high school and could barely read. He had fallen through the education cracks but, somehow, he managed to get into the US Air Force.

At the age of 23, the man described as 'the toughest man alive' looked a lot different to what he does now. He had left the Air Force and was working a job as a pest controller. The combination of stress-eating, depression and low self-esteem saw him blow out to 297 pounds (135 kilograms). By his own admission, he was fat, lazy and miserable.

An ad on TV for the Navy SEALs sparked something in him, and he decided to apply. The recruiter explained that at his height he could not weigh more than 191 pounds (91 kilograms) to be eligible, and that he'd need to drop 100 pounds in less than three months if he wanted in.

Challenge accepted!

Goggins had to get curious about a few of his habits – most importantly, his habit of living in his comfort zone. Being comfortable is a curious habit: it's useful until it's not.

Becoming a Navy SEAL was the bigger, better offer that inspired him to flick his discipline switch and transform his mind, body and spirit. He dropped the kilos and made it into SEAL training.

Neuroscience guru Dr Andrew Huberman coined the term 'limbic friction'. It describes the resistance the New Brain has to overcome to get the Old Brain on board with the habit change. Eating donuts has very little limbic friction – it's easy to do, particularly if you dig donuts. Dragging a 300-pound body off the couch and running five miles (when you are spectacularly unfit) is the opposite. It takes a lot of cognitive control and top-down effort from the New Brain to convince the Old Brain that the discomfort of bouncing your lazy arse for five miles is worth it. Remember, action has to go through the emotion-driven Old Brain, and your New Brain needs to get really **curious and persuasive** if you are going to change what you do.

Goggins has a way of dealing with the pain of habit change that is as effective as it is counterintuitive. He has found a way to get a dopamine hit from doing something that's difficult. His advice: 'Embrace the pain'. In other words, get comfortable with the discomfort and use all the mind tools at your disposal to SWAP the habits that aren't helping.

Doing the grunt work

Mental grunt work is the effort it takes to get curious, decide on the thing you are going to do and bear with the pain while you do it. It's the hard bit that has to be done if you are going to be committed to change, rather than just interested in it. I know I'm starting to rattle off more macho clichés than a beer ad, but the thing about clichés is that they are repeated because they are true.

There's a Buddhist saying (often attributed to His Holiness the Dalai Lama), **'Pain is inevitable, suffering is optional'**.

It's true: the grunt work of habit change can be really painful:

- Starting an exercise routine when you are 136 kilograms (300 pounds) and depressed is painful.
- Leaving a successful career and following your passion hurts, especially when you feel like you are failing.
- Facing up to your demons and insecurities that are causing anxiety is scary and chock-full of pain.
- Breaking the habit of micromanaging your team at work and allowing them freedom can be hard.
- The new computer system at work should be awesome, but at the moment, I hate it.

Change will always involve some mental pain. Stress and suffering are optional, though.

The grunt work happens when you're right at the beginning of a new, deliberate habit loop to replace an old one that doesn't serve you (see Figure 4.1). It's like the first trek across the overgrown sand dunes to create a new path, or the first time you drive a car: it takes mental effort, cognitive control, top-down thinking, New Brain override… whatever you want to call it. It is the heavy-lifting part of habit change!

Figure 4.1: Grunt work

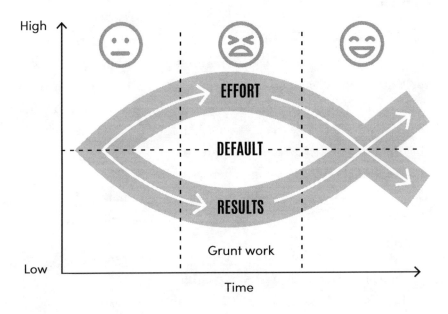

When you're in the grunt work stage, you often get worse results from more effort initially. It becomes really tempting to go back to the familiar and take the path of least resistance. This is the point where you've got to channel your inner Goggins. In *Can't Hurt Me* he urges: **'Don't let your body or mind do exactly what it wants to do! Take control!'**

What the gravel-voiced Navy SEAL is saying is: do the grunt work. Don't let your inner sea squirt run the show. Reframe your curious habits to incorporate your bigger, better offer, enjoy your small wins and learn from the losses.

Comfort isn't joy

My friend Michael DeSanti runs gratitude training workshops and wrote a book called *New Man Emerging*. Mike agrees that parking yourself in your comfort zone for any length of time is a curious habit: **'Rarely do we reflect on the prices that we pay by living within those comfort zones only to find how truly uncomfortable our comfort zone is'.**

He says that people often think they want comfort. If comfort is your goal, you can get comfort. But you have to know that comfort isn't joy. Comfort isn't achievement, satisfaction, growth or living a full life. Comfort is comfort. All of those other things lie on the other side of discomfort.

It's really comfortable to lay on the couch and binge-watch *Game of Thrones*, but if you want to live a full life, eventually you need to turn off the other-world soft porn and work out a way to get uncomfortable. To be alive is to feel discomfort, to be constantly growing and changing. There is no change without a little bit of pain.

David Goggins has mastered getting out of his comfort zone. In his 20-plus years in the military, he served in Iraq and Afghanistan, and he is the only person in the US Armed Forces to complete SEAL training (including two Hell Weeks), the Army Ranger School and Air Force Tactical Air Control training.

After retiring from the military in 2015, he started running ultramarathons, competing in long-distance cycling events and writing his book. He has helped millions of people to get curious, to step out of their comfortable default loops and into a place where they can thrive.

Goggins made an art form out of discomfort. To paraphrase Robert Frost, he took the habit loop less travelled and it made all the difference.

Regrets, I've had a few

Which is the more uncomfortable thought for you: to stay still, keep going as you are and be in a similar spot this time next year, or to do something difficult, get out of your comfort zone and risk humiliation and failure?

Three years ago, I invented an ergonomic chair. My back would get sore when I was sitting all day, and so I came up with a way to strengthen my core while sitting. It was called a 'Jellyfish Chair'. Nothing too complicated – just a bosu ball (imagine a big, bouncy fit-ball cut in half) on a stool. It was awesome. The chair helped me engage my core and fixed my bad back. I thought, 'Everyone needs these, and I'm going to sell millions of them online'. I enrolled in an online course on how to sell products on Amazon, and I found a manufacturer in Taiwan. We got 2000 chairs made and shipped them to Australia and to Amazon in the USA. 'Look out offices everywhere, Jellyfish Chairs are coming to revolutionise where you plant your butt!'

The manufacturer I'd found in Taiwan – not the most ethical dude in the world – thought my idea was great. Despite signing a non-disclosure agreement, he stole my design and sold exclusive rights to *my* chair to a rival company in the States. When my container-load of chairs was completed, he refused to send them to the USA because he had an exclusive deal with my competitors. I had to send the chairs to China, repack them and re-route them to Amazon in the US.

In this process, half the balls went flat, and my reviews on Amazon were less than flattering. I was spending hours each day dealing with customer complaints, and it sucked.

The Jellyfish Chair was a flop. Great idea but terribly executed (mostly because I am a bit too trusting and think everyone will do the right thing).

My friend Kevin gave me some great advice: 'If you have to eat shit, *don't nibble*'. Like in the Kenny Rogers song 'The Gambler', you've gotta know when to hold 'em and when to fold 'em.

I sold off the remaining stock and cut my losses.

Trying to sell a new, unique product with worldwide logistical issues and less-than-ethical manufacturers was stressful. I was way out of my comfort zone, and it cost me a few thousand dollars. It was a pain in the arse, even though the chairs were comfy.

Would I do it again? Abso-effing-lutely!

The small amount of money I lost was 'school fees'. I learned a lot and gave it a crack. It was exciting to get out of my comfort zone, and I'm glad I was brave enough to give it a try.

Whenever outcomes are uncertain, scary or difficult to predict, the brain likes to revert to the status quo as the default option. You do nothing, you don't change. Fear of failure is real, and it causes inertia and stops people trying.

Why do we fear failure so much? For many of us, it has a lot to do with worrying about what other people will think. I love this old saying: **What other people think of you is none of your business.**

In my own experience, and working with others as a coach, I have noticed that fear of failure has a lot to do with what *you* think of you. If you have a strong sense of self-worth, failing at something won't change that. You will see it as a learning experience.

Remember, human motivation has three drivers: avoid pain, seek pleasure and conserve energy (the easy path). In the short term, staying as you are is safe and easy. It ticks two of the three boxes. The problem with the status quo? What is easy and safe now will always bite you in the bum via boredom and the regret of not trying.

Avoiding the stress of change is like the instant gratification of credit cards: you get what is easy now, but you'll have to pay for it later.

You might have heard about Australian palliative care nurse Bronnie Ware, who did a study of elderly people and their top five regrets. They were:

1. I wish I'd pursued my dreams and aspirations.
2. I wish I hadn't worked so hard.
3. I wish I'd had the courage to speak my mind.
4. I wish I'd stayed in touch with friends.
5. I wish I'd let myself be happier.

There are a whole bunch of curious habits right there.

Number one on this list is all about regretting staying with the status quo, not being brave enough to have a crack.

Trying and failing is never that bad. It may feel stressful at the time, but lessons are learned and life goes on.

My dreams of revolutionising offices everywhere may not have come to fruition, but I helped cement my identity as someone who is brave and has a go. There will be no regrets about Jellyfish Chairs when I'm on my deathbed. Maybe a few laughs though.

Let's get curious

- What grunt work are you dodging?
- Where in your life are you getting uncomfortable with the status quo?
- What is the thing you will regret *not* doing?

Chapter 5

Expecting perfection

'Perfectionism is a dream killer, because it's just
fear disguised as trying to do your best.'
– Mastin Kipp

It's 9.30 p.m. on a Saturday night, and Summer is already home and curled up on the couch with a blanket and a warm drink. Her first night out in months ended early when a familiar tightness in her stomach turned into the full-blown constriction that happens when she gets really anxious and her inner sea squirt wants out of there *now*. It wasn't a panic attack, but it was pretty damn close.

Summer has always been a high achiever – the kid who was told how smart she was and did her best to live up to that reputation. She had the little blip in grade 9 when her straight As at school started giving way to a sprinkling of Bs and the occasional C, putting her identity as the brainiac in danger. At this point she realised natural intelligence will only get you so far, and you actually have to do the work to get the marks.

As with most teenagers, Summer dealt with upheavals in her social circles. Friends were lost and others gained. Putting the social turmoil aside, she dug in, did the grunt work and finished school (and university) in her rightful place near the top of the class. High marks felt good, so her brain thought, 'Let's do that again'. B.F. Skinner would be proud.

As we know, a curious habit is something we feel, think or do where our default no longer helps. Summer's habit of expecting high marks and doing the work to get them was helpful. Arranging her time to optimise output was a helpful habit as well. So why was this smart and engaging 21-year-old with lots of friends getting so anxious that she had to go home on a Saturday night and snuggle up in her Oodie?

The answer lies in two factors that feed each other: expectation and perfectionism. Summer had both of them, and they were feeding the anxiety monster.

Expectation breeds resentment

Like many curious habits, perfectionism starts out as a good thing (attention to detail) and is helpful until it's not. It ticks all the boxes for initial high performance; but, as Summer found out, expecting perfection quickly becomes a burden and doesn't always lead to a well-rounded, happy and balanced life.

Summer likes to be in control. It feels safe, and her inner sea squirt can relax and calm the farm when everything is in order. The anxiety came when she went out. Her friends liked to party, and like most freshly minted adults in the Western world, they embraced booze and doing stupid shit. Drinking and acting out made Summer feel like she was out of control, which did nothing for her rising anxiety levels. She would get so stressed by her friends' antics that her fight-or-flight system would kick into overdrive, and she would run to the safety of the couch.

Summer's expectations of her friends' behaviour were making the situation worse. She wanted her friends to stop getting loose and behaving like drunken idiots – but her mates had no intention of living up to her standards. At the same time, she felt her friends had expectations of her that involved sculling Vodka Cruisers and letting her hair down. She was comfortable with her hair exactly how it was.

There is an old saying: 'Expectations are resentments in advance'. This is exactly how it was for Summer. The combined stress of her expectations of herself and those she was imposing on her friends had her anxiety meter stuck in the red zone. Her inner sea squirt gave her a convenient option: stay home, and you won't have to deal with this anxiety or feel the resentments that are brewing. Hello social anxiety, where's my Oodie?

I'm very good friends with Summer's mum and dad. One night, Summer and I got talking. She explained that she was avoiding social situations and was feeling a bit highly strung. We arranged for her to come and have a coaching session the next week, and we unpacked a few of the things that were going on for her.

Finding Carlos

I think you'd like Carlos; I know I do. It's taken me a long time to get to know him, and occasionally he can be a bit elusive, but Carlos is awesome once you find him.

One of the tools I've developed in my coaching practice is called 'Finding Carlos'. It's a process of identifying the characteristics of your best self. I call these your 'identity goals', because they describe the type of person you aspire to be. Identity goals are:

- **Intrinsic:** They come from inside and are not about external achievements or validation.
- **Intentional:** You do them on purpose, and they are deliberate.

- **Infinite:** You can never fully achieve these goals and will always need to keep working on them. You want to be aspiring to these same traits when you are 90 years old.

Carlos is the better version of me. Luke is a bit lazy, easily distracted and can be a little inconsiderate. Luke might step over a bit of rubbish on the street; Carlos would pick it up and put it in the bin. The reason I like Carlos so much is that he is super-clear about what is important. Carlos knows his identity goals.

My identity goals are to be: **curious, creative and generous**.

If I am living up to those three goals, I am as happy as a pig in mud. This is why I love running workshops and coaching: they provide the perfect opportunity for me to be curious, creative and generous.

I coached Summer through the Finding Carlos process and we unpacked a lot of the fears and worries that were tying her in knots. We talked about the pressure of study and her need to excel. She explained the issues with peer pressure and how uncomfortable she was with her friends not doing what she perceived as 'the right thing'. She also realised that her long-term boyfriend was treating her more like a mother than a partner. All of these things had her stress bucket full to the brim, and something had to give.

When we finished the session, Summer clearly understood what habit loops she had to change and who she wanted to be. She had listed her identity goals as: **'brave and determined with a thoughtful acceptance'**.

The first two were the ABCs of her. Being brave and determined were traits she had inherited from her mum and were default characteristics, and she liked them. Developing 'thoughtful acceptance' was the bit she had to work on.

In chapter 3 we talked about the habits SWAP, the first step of which is to be SELECTIVE: selecting a new habit or trait, and being clear about the desired reward. By selecting 'thoughtful acceptance', she had a clear view of who she wanted to be and what the better version of herself looked like.

Striving to be your best self is healthy and essential for a happy and fulfilling life. Expecting perfection from yourself and others is another thing altogether. The last person you want to be resenting is yourself. In chapter 1 we talked about addiction being a progressive narrowing of things that bring you joy, and continuing to do something despite adverse consequences. I think perfectionism ticks both these boxes.

Dr Brené Brown, University of Houston shame researcher and badass guru of all things human, defined perfectionism as:

'...a self-destructive and addictive belief system that fuels this primary thought: "If I look perfect, live perfectly, work perfectly, and do everything perfectly, I can avoid or minimise the painful feelings of shame, judgement, and blame".'

So perfectionism, according to Dr Brown, is a way to dodge negative emotions. Shame, judgement and blame don't feel good. If I look perfect, get perfect marks and have a perfectly arranged sock drawer, then nobody can say anything bad about me. Dr Brown also describes perfectionism as a '20 tonne shield' that people carry around to protect themselves from thoughts and feelings they don't want. Like all curious habits, the shield helped at some stage – but it eventually became heavy.

Perfectionism kills curiosity. It turns failures and mistakes into personal defects that make you feel like shit. If you have to be perfect to feel good about yourself, you are not going to try new things, because of the risk of failure and a potentially huge hit to your self-worth.

Within weeks of our session, Summer had ended a relationship that had passed its used-by date, and rediscovered the joy of connecting with friends. She learned to put the shield down. She realised her friends weren't perfect, and no matter how good her marks were or how hard she studied, neither was she.

Summer now has options, particularly in social situations. Things that would typically trigger anxiety are now cues to get curious. Curiosity lets her connect with the part of herself that is brave and determined, with a thoughtful acceptance.

Anxiety is your brain and body asking you to pay attention. Having thoughtful acceptance helps Summer reassure herself that everything is OK. Striving for excellence is an admirable quality, and Summer continues to do that. She is currently studying to be a doctor and killing it. She is brave and determined (as always), and her new-found thoughtful acceptance has emptied expectations and perfectionism from her stress bucket and exchanged it for curiosity. It's good being Summer!

Let's get curious

- Where is expecting perfection holding you back?
- What character trait do you need to get curious about?
- Finish this sentence: 'It's good being me because I am...'

Chapter 6

Procrastination – I'll think about my habits tomorrow

'Why do today what you can put off 'til tomorrow?'
– SpongeBob SquarePants

I have a curious habit of procrastinating. No, bugger it, we *all* have a curious habit of procrastinating. In my research for this book, I asked a heap of people about their curious habits, and procrastination was top of a lot of people's lists. We don't all do it in the same way or for exactly the same reasons, but we all procrastinate. Some of us just tell ourselves better stories about why it's OK.

Procrastination is all about regulating your emotions. If something is stressful or annoying, putting it off until later will give you the instant gratification of feeling better. The thing still needs to be done, but that's a problem for 'future you'.

There are two main types of procrastination that depend on the task we are putting off: tasks with deadlines and tasks without.

Anyone who has ever had a deadline knows what a powerful motivator a looming date on the calendar can be. In his TED Talk

'Inside the mind of the master procrastinator', Tim Urban describes the panic monster: the scary beast that comes alive when a deadline approaches to inspire focused work. The panic monster increases the stress levels to get you motivated and on task. Without the stress of the panic monster, many of us could procrastinate forever. Stress from deadlines gets us moving; it gives us motivation.

I hate doing my tax. Every year, I say to myself that I'm going to do it on 1 July, and every year it ends up limping to the accountant (half done) in March or April. Benjamin Franklin summed it up when he said, 'In this world nothing can be said to be certain, except death and taxes'. I'm in no hurry to do either. Avoiding death is *not* a curious habit – avoiding death is evolutionarily prudent and advisable. Procrastinating about filling in a few forms, attaching some receipts to an email and forwarding it to the accountant is a curious habit. I hate doing accounts, paperwork bores me senseless and paying tax sucks. Nothing about doing tax feels good, and my inner sea squirt tells me to avoid it.

Remember, emotion drives action. When we allow our inner sea squirt to run the show, we avoid pain, seek pleasure and take the path of least resistance. Procrastination happens when the thought of doing something difficult (such as your tax) feels like pain, so we avoid it and move toward something that feels like joy (such as, well, anything else). The hassle is that it needs to get done. In the nine months between the end of the financial year and the deadline to submit my return, I would have thought about doing it 100 times. That's 100 little squirts of stress that could have been avoided with an hour or two of annoyance on 1 July.

I can hear the pre-crastinators (it's not a word, but you know who you are) of the world burring up about now. Those people who do their tax on 1 July, pay every bill the moment they get it and have perfectly organised sock drawers. 'I don't procrastinate!' the organised ones say as they tick things off their to-do lists with joyous satisfaction. Deadlines are never a worry for the pre-crastinators, because getting something done feels great to them and they hate a task to hang over their heads. It's still sea squirt mode, it's just a bit more efficient.

So, if some people are great at getting things done straight away, how can we call them procrastinators? That's where the non-deadline-related procrastination comes into it.

Here are a few examples of non-deadline procrastination:

· The trip around Australia that you haven't gotten around to
· Asking out Jane from accounts (who you've been crushing on for years)
· Writing that screenplay about the stripper/welder who wants to be a ballerina
· Singing 'I Will Survive' at karaoke while wearing a leopard-print bodysuit
· Launching your own range of designer dog collars
· The goat yoga business that has been put on hold for five years
· Writing the book about procrastination.

My friend and author Alicia McKay calls this type of procrastination 'caravanning'. Her parents have been threatening to buy a caravan and take off for years. Between businesses and grandkids, it's not going to happen, but they keep torturing themselves by going to caravan shows and looking at websites about motorhomes. If you are going to do it, do it! If not, stop dangling the dream like a carrot on a stick. We all procrastinate about something, but having the self-awareness to admit it and decide whether we *really* want to go caravanning is the key to mastering non-deadline-related procrastination.

Without deadlines and Tim Urban's 'panic monster', it is easy to procrastinate forever.

Why we procrastinate

Nineteenth-century German philosopher Arthur Schopenhauer isn't renowned for being the most light-hearted, optimistic fellow; he is famous for being insightful, despite having a somewhat pessimistic view of the world. He said: **'Life swings like a pendulum backward and forward between pain and boredom'**.

I'm not one to dwell on the thinkings of dead pessimists, but this quote got my attention.

We have all felt the awesome feeling of being in flow – that zone where your mind is focused on the task and time becomes irrelevant while you do your best work.

It turns out our 19th-century German friend was onto something. If you look at it from a stress point of view, boredom is not enough stress, and pain is too much. The balance between the two is where we find flow.

Our stress hormones have evolved to get us to move (do something) or protect ourselves. In short, not enough stress means we're not motivated to move; we procrastinate. (This is 'boredom' to Schopenhauer.)

Introducing a small amount of stress is a good way to deal with the curious habit of procrastination. Setting deadlines, making commitments to yourself and recruiting accountability partners are all ways to introduce some stress to ensure you take action.

Motivation: I'll get started when...

How many ducks do you need to line up before you start doing the thing you were born to do? You know, that thing that will change your life and make the world a better place?

Fear, perfectionism and imposter syndrome all feed into the procrastination habit. 'Once I get another few ducks in a row, then I will share my work with the world.'

I am not comfortable in front of a camera (I have a great head for radio). But when COVID-19 killed in-person events, I realised that if I was going to share my message with the world, it would have to be on Zoom and in videos. I bought lights, a new camera and a switchbox to change cameras. The plan was, once I got all the stuff, I'd run a webinar. For months I collected gear and put off actually using it, until finally I just ran the webinar. It went really well, and I used about half the equipment I thought I 'needed' to do a good job.

The lesson is this: just do it! Try, fail and learn, and before you know it, you'll have broken the shackles of inertia. Sometimes you just need to get comfortable with discomfort and do the thing that scares you.

A mother duck doesn't arrange her ducklings – she just starts walking, and the ducks follow; that's how they get in line. Action gives you answers.

Getting crystal clear on what you want and making the bigger, better offer so compelling that your inner sea squirt gets on board to make it happen is the key to finding motivation.

People are like big ships: it takes a lot of effort to make them change direction. Procrastinating keeps the ship going in the same direction.

A pharmaceutical company once wanted to convince its mail-order customers to change from branded medication to generic medication. Same drugs, just cheaper and in a different package. The customers would need to give permission to the pharmaceutical company before being switched to generic brands. The company sent out letters asking customers to change, noting that they would save a significant amount of money. Three percent of people changed. The new medications were just as effective and less than half the cost, yet only 3 percent of people opted to change.

The company decided to up the ante and offered *free* medication for a year if customers switched. Only about 10 percent of customers changed.

Next, the company decided to do something drastic. They sent a letter to say that they would *stop* sending the meds unless the customer replied to the letter with the answer to one simple question: 'Do you want generic medication, or branded medication that will cost you twice as much?'

Dan Ariely, psychologist and author of the book *Predictably Irrational*, describes this as putting a T-intersection in the decision road. You have to do something when you get to a T-intersection: you can't keep procrastinating.

Once people were forced to make a deliberate choice and not just keep going in the same direction, they were more likely to change: 80 percent of people switched to the generic medication and saved themselves and the pharmaceutical company money.

Procrastination is a curious habit that's about regulating emotions and fear of the unknown. People often will choose a known *bad* outcome over an unknown outcome that may end up being fantastic: think applying for a new job, leaving an abusive partner, joining a new gym or starting a new podcast. We avoid the pain of uncertainty and the regret of making a bad choice. Unfortunately, inertia leaves us stuck with the same habits forever.

What about the other side of the pendulum swing – Schopenhauer's pain?

Legendary Australian football coach John Kennedy once delivered a famous quote during his three-quarter-time Grand Final address to his losing players: '**Your psychological limit is a lot closer than your physical limit. Remember when you're tired, and you think you can't go any further, you can!**'

From an evolutionary point of view, Kennedy's observation makes perfect sense. If you were a caveman running through the Serengeti, you would want your psychological limit to be lower than your physical limit. Running until you passed out would make you dinner for any lazy sabre-toothed tiger who happened to be passing by. Evolution has ensured that the stress of pain (or the pain of stress) makes us give up mentally before being unable to move physically. This is why we quit (see Figure 6.1).

Figure 6.1: The 'gets shit done' zone

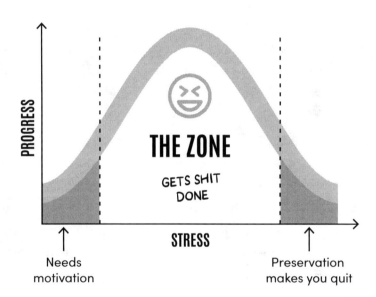

Stanford neuroscientist Dr Andrew Huberman has an interesting take on why we quit and how to keep going. If we look at stress hormones, we see that they rise in the morning to get us started. If this doesn't happen, we wouldn't get out of bed (the ultimate procrastination). This is one end of Schopenhauer's pendulum. The other end is what happens when the events of the day cause our stress levels to rise uncomfortably. If they get too high, we quit.

To increase resilience, Dr Huberman says we need to recruit our reward system – dopamine. Dopamine, our 'drive to thrive' hormone, has a buffering effect on stress. It knocks stress levels down and delays the need to give up and quit. Setting small, achievable goals and celebrating reaching them will increase dopamine, decrease stress and delay the urge to quit. Ultramarathon runners call this 'thin-slicing' your goals. Don't think of the finish line; just get to the next lamppost, celebrate that win (sunshine) and set a new thin-sliced goal. Huberman recommends a system he calls DPO: Duration, Path, Outcome. Set a time, make a plan and have a desired outcome. This creates small goals throughout the day, and when we hit those goals and celebrate, this will decrease our stress levels. Without having small wins throughout your day, whatever you are doing appears futile, and doing something with no purpose *adds* to your stress levels and increases your chances of quitting.

Imagine stress is like filling your petrol tank. When the tank is full, the pump cuts off. It quits. Celebrating small wins increases the size of the tank and enables you to continue and thrive under pressure.

The other thing you can do to stop yourself quitting early is to reframe how you think about the discomfort of stress. Get comfortable with discomfort, and get curious. Stress is a data point that is there to make you pay attention. Seeing stress as a positive thing and something that is there to help will improve your resilience. By finding purpose and reframing stress from a threat to a challenge, we can utilise it to help achieve our goals. Reframing stress, in effect, pushes the quit line to the right and gives us a bigger zone.

Procrastinate on purpose

Our goal is to stay between the motivation and preservation lines we saw on Figure 6.1.

When you are feeling like your brain is cooked, however, you need to take a break, and that is where deliberate procrastination is needed.

Imagine you have a stress bucket: an amount of stress that you can endure before you quit. When you are starting to feel overwhelmed, but before your brain turns into a ball of goo, it's a good idea to empty some stress hormones out of your bucket.

Take a walk, do some exercise in nature, or even watch a comedy video on YouTube. All of these things will empty some stress out of your bucket and let you get back to whatever you are doing with enthusiasm and some bandwidth to keep learning.

Don't reach for your phone as a way of recharging, though. A recent study from Tel Aviv University and the University of Michigan measured anxiety levels in their 68 subjects and found that using social media as a form of procrastination caused increased anxiety. It appears that using social media as your procrastination tool of choice doesn't empty your bucket. If you do manage to get back to work after a scrolling binge, the studies show that your concentration will be worse, and you will tap out and quit more quickly.

As a time-wasting procrastination tool, social media is awesome. Features such as infinite scroll allow you to keep rolling through content forever. As a way to empty your bucket and refresh, though, it's terrible.

The trick with deliberate procrastination, just like anything difficult or stressful, is to use Huberman's DPO model and specify a duration, path and outcome. For example: 'For the next 30 minutes, I'm going to walk the dog, listen to music or watch funny cat videos on YouTube. I know those things empty my stress bucket. After that, I'm going to nail section four of my English assignment'.

Going back to Schopenhauer's swing between pain and boredom, I think we can learn something about procrastinating on purpose and embracing the boredom end of the swing. Think about kids on a swing. Hold a child's feet at the end of a swing and they squeal with joy. Keep them there for too long and they cry.

We *have to* swing, and the higher we go at one end, the higher we need to go at the other.

Dr Adam Fraser is an organisational psychology researcher from Deakin University. He was studying resilience levels and found something quite profound in the data. It's not that we have a problem with resilience; it's that we don't put enough effort into our recovery. He said: 'We don't have a resilience problem, we have a recovery problem'.

Be as specific with your downtime as you are with your work. You need to deliberately let yourself swing to the chilled-out end of the arc and recover with as much purpose as you work. By being specific with your duration, path and outcome of recharging, you can free up some room in your bucket to keep going.

Getting curious about procrastination can help you get more done with less hassle. You'll learn to notice when you're procrastinating on purpose versus using it as an avoidance strategy. It might be as simple as asking what your inner sea squirt is trying to get out of it. Curiosity makes the unknown known.

Let's get curious

- What's your procrastination tool of choice?
- What are your non-deadline procrastinations?
- Next time you feel agitated and your bucket is full, what deliberate form of procrastination will you choose to calm the farm? (Remember duration, path and outcome.)

Chapter 7

Self-talk that sucks

'The voice in my head is an asshole'
– Dan Harris

Internal dialogue is a quirk of human nature. It's like having an internal narrator chattering away in your head. Unfortunately, most people's narrator is a bit like Statler and Waldorf, those cranky old bastards from *The Muppets*, best known for their cantankerous opinions and shared penchant for heckling. Just like Dan Harris, my internal narrator can be a bit of a dick.

The human brain, particularly the New Brain, is a prediction machine. We anticipate what's going to happen, and that gives us options around what to do. The problem comes when our inner sea squirt gets involved. Our Old Brain has a negative bias, meaning that it has a tendency to take more notice of threats than it does rewards. Prehistoric humans could miss out on something good, and they would survive to hunt and gather another day. If they didn't notice a tiger, they became its lunch and no longer took any part in the evolution process. The ones who took notice of the bad stuff survived. Our negative bias makes sense, but why does that make my inner voice a dickhead?

Like most dickheads, the voice in your head likes to always be right. Say, for example, you have to reverse into a really tight car park. Your brain will assess the size of the spot. It will then quickly bring up memories of similar situations in the past and decide whether it can be done. If you consider yourself to be the Jason Statham of reverse parking, the narrator is on your side. If there is a whole bunch of traffic about, you're running late and you have a dodgy history of scraping wheel rims and damaging bumper bars, your internal narrator will be more like the cranky muppets.

Here is where it gets interesting. If we stuff up the tricky parking manoeuvre and fail, our internal narrator throws in a little 'I told you so' – so we may have failed in our attempt to squeeze into the parking space, but at least we were *right*! It's a weird quirk of human nature that we love to be right even when the results aren't desirable, don't help and leave us worse off.

Know who's talking

Dr Amy Silver is a psychologist and the author of the book *The Loudest Guest*. She describes self-talk as a party that's going on in our head, and *fear* is the loudest guest. Fear dominates conversations and can be heard across the room. I spoke to Amy about self-talk and why we aren't nicer to ourselves. She explained that the fear voice in our head gets louder the more we push it away; but if we lean into it and understand what the fear is trying to protect us from, it has less power over us. Fear is like a toddler: the more you try and ignore it, the louder it gets. Amy's advice is to make sure you acknowledge fear, but don't let it control you – it gets a seat at the table, but it doesn't get a vote on what you do.

Knowing who's telling your narration story matters. Understanding that fear is talking decreases its power. It's a bit like the Disney animated movie *Inside Out*, which delightfully depicts the different human emotions as characters that are controlling things inside the protagonist's head. In the movie, you knew when Joy, Sadness, Anger, Fear or Disgust was running the show. Understanding that the voice in your head can be a dick sometimes helps, too.

University of Michigan professor Dr Ethan Kross and his colleagues did an insightful experiment into self-talk. They hooked participants up to EEG machines, which showed the parts of their brains that were activated. The participants were asked to look at disturbing photographs and explain how the images made them feel using first-person language ('I feel…') and third-person language ('Luke feels…'). The EEG showed that referring to yourself in the third person moves activity away from the emotional and reactive Old Brain and out to the thoughtful and logical New Brain. In other words, simply putting some distance between yourself and what you're feeling lets your New Brain take over and apply logic to the situation. It's a way to talk back to your negative self-talk.

In the Bible, there is a story of King Solomon, who was a wise and noble leader who became king of the Jewish people. As king, he was known for giving great advice, and people came from distant lands to seek his counsel. The problem was that his own life was a mess. He had problems with wives and money and couldn't sort out his own shit. He was great at solving other people's problems, but his own backyard was a mess.

Being able to give great advice but not being able to sort out your own shit is a curious habit that has become known as 'Solomon's Paradox'. It essentially means that **people are wiser when they reason about others' problems**. It's easy to give good advice to others, but it is harder to know what to do about your own problems. Using third-person language or an alter ego creates distance between yourself and the problem. Being able to create distance allows you to connect your Old and New Brains and make King Solomon proud.

How does the best you sound?

Back in chapter 5 I introduced Carlos, my alter ego. Carlos helps me reframe the self-talk that doesn't help. As Luke, I can be a bit judgy and critical about myself, whereas Carlos is a pretty positive dude who is a far more encouraging narrator while still remaining curious. Using an alter ego like this can be a really effective way to recruit your inner narrator to work for you, rather than being the Nostradamus of future stuff-ups.

If you are going to improve your self-talk, it's good to know what the best version of you sounds like. To improve your conversations with yourself, you need to find and focus on the characteristics of the best version of you.

Another mentor of mine, Matt Church, has a process he calls 'Buddha's delight' (not the vegetarian dish), and it's all about **'Recognising your good qualities in someone else and delighting in the discovery'**.

I use this concept to help people get out of their own head, create some distance and look objectively at the qualities they admire in other people that they also see in themselves. I ask them to pick three people and list the characteristics about them that they admire:

- A person from their tribe (a friend or family member)
- Someone from history
- A character from a book or a movie.

I also ask my clients to think of a time in their life when they were at their best, and describe themselves then. We do this last, and it is where the magic happens. Almost without fail, people pick a time when they encountered difficulties and challenges – when shit got hard. Great sailors need rough seas, and the best version of yourself rarely comes out when everything is rosy.

By this time, my client has a list of characteristics that they admire in themselves and other people. They then choose three or four of the most important traits, and they become their identity goals (which I talked about in chapter 5). Remember, these characteristics need to be:

- Intrinsic (they are not about outside achievements)
- Intentional (you chose these traits deliberately)
- Infinite (you never completely achieve them).

Identity goals are my way of living intentionally. Jay Shetty, in his book *Think like a Monk*, describes it as, '**Stepping back from external goals, letting go of outward definitions of success, and looking within**'.

My friend Dr Craig Duncan, a mindset guru, says identity goals form part of your 'deathbed scorecard'. If you could only put three or four words to describe you on your tombstone, what would they be?

It's never too young to start defining your good characteristics. Back in 2012, when my daughter was only 10, we had a conversation that has resonated with both of us ever since. I asked her, 'What's the best thing about being you?' She tilted her head to the side and got that curious look on her face that little kids get. And she said, 'I'm really good at trying, even when I'm not very good at something and things get really difficult. I still keep going. And I might not ever be the best, but I always keep going'.

My response: 'That means you're tenacious; that's fantastic. And what other things are good about being you?'

After thinking some more, she said, 'I'm really good at noticing when there's something wrong with other people. I can always tell when something's not quite right, particularly if they haven't got any friends at lunch, or something like that. I always go and sit with them and usually make them feel better'.

My heart swelled and I got that big warm, fuzzy serotonin squirt that parents get when they see something beautiful in their kids. I said, 'That's beautiful, Chloe; that means you have empathy.'

I look at parenting our daughter (even now she's a young adult) with such pride and think, yeah, I can probably take some of the credit for that. My wife can certainly take a lot more. But most of it has come from Chloe. That simple conversation made her aware of her superpowers of tenacity and empathy, and she has built on them even more over the years since.

Feeding your nemesis

Every superhero needs a nemesis. Superman had Lex Luthor, Batman had the Joker and Austin Powers had Dr. Evil – and the Carlos in your head needs one, too.

Carlos has a nemesis, and his name is Little Luke. He is the uncoordinated little pigeon-toed kid from Nerang (the dodgy part) who couldn't read until grade 9 and had to try so much harder than everyone else to become acceptably mediocre at anything. While Carlos will try anything, Little Luke is a lot more cautious, and will chime in with reminders of reasons something can't be done and why he's not good enough. Carlos has dreams and loves a challenge; Little Luke has excuses and threats, and wants me to stay safe and small in his comfort zone.

Carlos wants to write books, run Stress RESET programs and help people take the toxic stress out of life. Carlos has a message to share; he believes in himself and is curious, creative and generous about what he can do. Little Luke often asks, 'Who are you to do that? Why would anyone listen to you?' His advice is to keep doing the safe job, stay small and *not* do the things that light me (and Carlos) up.

A colleague of mine from corporate life, Darrel, was the best negotiator I've ever known. I once asked how he always manages to come out on top in negotiations. He told me he has a simple strategy: 'Find out what people want and show them how they can live without it'.

Little Luke utilises Darrel's negotiation strategy. He points out all the things that could go wrong with Carlos' ideas and plans, and how much safer it is to stay put. If left to run the show, Little Luke will lock me into the safety of my comfort zone. Carlos tells me what I want, and Little Luke tells me how I can live without it. Curious habit?

Internal dialogue can be a bit like the old cartoons in which the hero has an angel on one shoulder and a devil on the other. Carlos and Little Luke are both perched on my shoulders, and the only way to make sure I'm talking to myself in a positive way is to be really clear about which one is doing the talking. If I recognise Little Luke, I can be pretty sure that what he's saying is straight from the sea squirt user manual.

You might be familiar with the story of the two wolves, sometimes attributed to the Cherokee people. It goes like this:

> A wise old man was talking to a boy and said, 'There are two wolves fighting inside of me. One is filled with anger, hate, shame, jealousy and lies. The other wolf is filled with love, joy, truth and peace. The battle rages inside of you and all men'.
>
> The boy thought for a moment and asked, 'Which wolf will win?'
>
> The old man answered: 'The one you feed'.

Imposter syndrome

Imposter syndrome is a collection of feelings of inadequacy that persist even in the face of evidence to the contrary. People with imposter syndrome experience chronic self-doubt and feel like frauds. Imposter syndrome can (and does) happen to just about anyone; and if you don't recognise it, call it out and look at it objectively, imposter syndrome will invade your self-talk like Genghis Khan rampaging his way through China. Just like Genghis Khan's army of Mongol invaders, imposter syndrome will aggressively kill any ambitions that don't align with staying small and safe with your familiar habits.

Wharton business school professor Adam Grant describes it like this:

Impostor syndrome is a paradox:

- Others believe in you.
- You don't believe in yourself.
- **Yet you believe yourself instead of them.**

If you doubt yourself, shouldn't you also doubt your judgement of yourself?

When multiple people believe in you, it might be time to believe them.

Research suggests that 70 percent of people have experienced imposter syndrome, and plenty of them are super-smart, successful and accomplished. Doubting yourself can make you try harder, be more thorough and dive deeper into areas to improve your skills. The problem occurs when imposter syndrome causes you to *not* try anything until you *know* you can do it perfectly.

Fear of failure, perfectionism, poor self-worth and fear of embarrassment are some of the many curious habits that build the foundation of imposter syndrome. Family dynamics and the beliefs you have as a kid play a big part in it, too. I have three older sisters who are all pretty smart. As a little kid, I had all sorts of problems reading and felt like the dunce of the family. I have a nerve missing in my left eye and would get double vision when I looked to the right. It had always been that way, and I didn't think to tell anyone that I saw two of things. The words would jumble, and I'd lose my place. I didn't read my first book until grade 9 (*To Kill a Mockingbird* – it's still a favourite) and only got through year 12 English with the help of my oldest sister. The story I told myself as a result of this was, 'I am no good at English'.

I wanted to write a book about leadership in my twenties, but imposter syndrome got the better of me, and I went back to the curious safety of my comfort zone and kept testing eyes.

The irony is that my work now revolves around books. I run a podcast called *Your Next Read*, in which I interview authors. I read at least a book a week and spend a lot of my time writing. This is my third book, and I still don't consider myself to be a writer. Imposter syndrome is tough to shift when your opinion of your abilities was formed when you were a kid. I'm grateful that you, the reader, have bought this book and have gotten this far. I'm even more grateful to my editor, Brooke, who somehow made my words legible. Imposter syndrome is all about the fear of not being good enough or being 'found out'.

Imposter syndrome decreases when you get **comfortable with discomfort** and learn to handle a bit of fear. Like Amy Silver said, **'Fear gets a seat at the table, but it doesn't get a vote in what you are going to do'.**

Feeling like an imposter sometimes is OK. If you have a habit loop that chooses inaction when confidence wanes, though, perhaps you could change that default to a deliberate habit of connecting to your inner Carlos and trying anyway. **Action gives you answers**, and doing is a good way of knowing if you can.

We all have **beliefs** that have somehow been transformed into **truths**. And as I always say, we are all making up stories in our own heads; if you are going to make things up for yourself to believe in, make things up that help.

Let's get curious

- What are the characteristics of the better version of you?
- What fears are stopping you?
- What stories are you making up that aren't helping?

Chapter 8

Toxic positivity and brutal optimism

'If no mistake you have made, yet losing you are…
a different game you should play.'
– Yoda

Let me tell you about Luke-land! It's a wonderful place where people are nice, everyone has the best intentions and friends look after each other. In Luke-land, optimism is the default, and we only see the silver linings – the cloud is barely visible and rarely even acknowledged. It's a wonderful place where everything always works out for the best and unicorns fart rainbows. Who wouldn't want to live there?

Like all curious habits, even optimism and positivity are useful until they're not. Seeing the good in people and assuming that everyone has positive intentions can help you build a happy life; the problem arises when that positivity blinds you to people and things that are negative or hurting you. Blind optimism makes the inner sea squirt happy. If you don't acknowledge the bad things that could possibly happen, the sea squirt is comfy and chilled.

The hassle is that 'negative' emotions like anger, disappointment and regret are great teachers. We are *meant* to feel them so we can understand more about the world. Unfortunately, when I'm living in Luke-land, I don't acknowledge my 'negative' emotions for long enough to learn the lessons they are trying to teach me.

There is an old saying that **the universe will keep hitting you with the same lessons until you learn them**.

Ignoring or brushing aside negative emotions has certainly forced me to learn a few tough lessons on more than one occasion. I've made really bad business decisions based on ego and the need to be the alpha-dude. Back when I was running a Specsavers practice, having the number-one practice in the country was really important to me. I remember going to a Specsavers awards night and being on a table where everyone got an award but me. I knew my store had the highest sales for the year, but there was no award for that. I was pissed, and I spoke to the operations manager the next day and had a whinge. Twenty-four hours later, a massive cake arrived at our shop with 'No.1 sales in Australia' written on it. The team was stoked, and I bullshitted myself that my protest was about them – but it wasn't. It was all about my ego.

When you're driven by ego, emotions like disappointment or anger can indicate that you aren't living by your values. Needing a clear perspex trophy to feel validated can be a cue that you need to improve self-awareness and get clear about your purpose. It took a few years for me to learn that lesson and get curious about negative emotions, rather than sweeping uncomfortable feelings under the rug and racing back to the comfort of Luke-land.

Emotions are what Harvard psychologist Dr Susan David calls 'signposts', as we learned in chapter 1. She rejects the concept of positive and negative emotions. She prefers to label them 'helpful' and 'unhelpful', and says they can change depending on the situation. In a threatening situation, anger can be very helpful. In a conversation with your spouse, it rarely helps.

Emotions like gratitude, trust and joy feel good. Sadness, disgust and rage aren't quite so pleasant. Rather than automatically trying to avoid these uncomfortable emotions, Dr David believes we need to lean into all of our emotions and get curious. By getting curious, we feel the emotion and put a space between what we feel and what we do.

Viktor Frankl, Holocaust survivor and psychiatrist who wrote the book *Man's Search for Meaning*, often has this quote attributed to him: **'Between stimulus and response there is a space. In that space is our power to choose our response'**.

Curiosity gives you space.

Without curiosity, our instinct is to move away from anything negative or painful and do whatever we can to decrease discomfort in the moment. When we get curious about what we are feeling, emotions become signposts and teach us important lessons about ourselves, our values and the world.

Dr David expands on a concept called 'toxic positivity' that was first coined in the '70s and explains the way that avoiding negative emotions can turn on you. She says when we continually deny our real emotions it makes us more fragile, because we're not living in the world as it is. We're living in a world as we wish it to be.

I think of toxic positivity as an inability to sit with the bad shit. It's the compulsive need to be in a happy, optimistic state in all situations. Unfortunately, the process of toxic positivity results in the denial, minimisation, and *invalidation* of the authentic human emotional experience.

If you ever have thoughts like these, get curious:

·   'It could be worse. At least it's not…'
·   'You shouldn't feel that way.'
·   'Don't think about it, just get on with it.'
·   'It's all in your mind, just think happy thoughts.'
·   'Happiness is a choice.'

None of these are inherently bad, and all of them have a time and a place.

Despite good intentions, indulging in toxic positivity can induce feelings of shame and cause people to bottle their negative emotions and bury their pain. In *Stress Teflon*, we made the case that without honest self-awareness, life gets more stressful. Toxic positivity is about trying to bullshit your way to feeling good without sitting with the uncomfortable emotions and learning their lessons.

Sometimes I wrestle with my dark emotions. Sometimes we snuggle.

Snuggling with your dark emotions improves self-awareness and ensures that the story you are telling yourself is a whole story, complete with the ugly, wobbly bits that need to be noticed.

Brutal optimism

Back in the '90s, a bunch of fitness crazes swept the nation, and the related equipment usually ended up gathering dust under the bed. Tae bo videos, the Ab Roller and rollerblading were all touted as the easy way to lose weight. My favourite craze was known as the Bowflex Eight-Minute At-Home Abs Workout. Some shirtless muppet with fluoro pink shorts and a sixpack would spend countless hours on late-night TV convincing you that your fitness goals would all come true if you bought these videos with a free set of steak knives – but only if you acted *now*. People all over the world put down their family-sized packs of potato chips and dialled the 1800 number to order the package so they could reveal their inner sixpacks in just eight minutes.

Late-night infomercials are filled with brutal optimism, which sucks people into the fantasy that all their problems can easily be solved with one purchase of anything from exercise equipment to the chop-o-matic. Marketers love to tout the latest technology that will help you do the hard thing (get a sixpack, launch a business or make a fortune in Bitcoin) with little or no effort. I call this the **'easy solution fallacy'**. The concept has started to creep into a lot of other parts of our thinking and has created a bunch of curious habits.

We've talked a lot about sea squirt mode in this book – the idea that our brains are designed to make us avoid pain and move towards pleasure. Our third motivator is to take the path of least resistance, and brutal optimism taps into that.

If you've ever looked at a difficult problem and said, 'All I have to do is…', you have probably bought into the easy solution fallacy. See if any of the following sound familiar:

· 'If I eat less and move more, I'll lose weight.'
· 'Just say no to drugs.'
· 'Always choose to be happy.'
· 'If you can dream it, you can do it.'
· 'Get great abs in just eight minutes a day!'

The problem with the easy solution fallacy is that if these things were easy, everyone would have a sixpack and a superyacht. Telling someone who is struggling with depression to 'just choose to be happy' is like telling an alcoholic to stop drinking or a morbidly obese person to eat less and do some exercise. Conditions like depression, addiction and obesity are really difficult problems to overcome. They have complex, deep-seated causes that can't be fixed with a few words that fit on a bumper sticker.

We see examples of brutal optimism all the time, and a lot of it comes in the form of well-meaning but simplistic advice. I have been guilty of dishing out this sort of advice to myself and other people. Saying things like 'Just do it this way' and 'Why don't you just think like this?' might appear to be helpful, but this type of advice rarely gets implemented or actioned because it doesn't give people the space to find the root cause of whatever the problem is.

The solution for me (both as a coach and in my own life) is to ask non-judgemental, curious questions like 'What am I getting out of this?' or 'What are my options here?' These questions, which often start with 'what', are about finding the real reason behind curious habits like overeating or imposter syndrome. 'Why' questions can be a bit judgy and shame-inducing, because you can't just stop the poor self-talk or resist whatever temptation is feeding your craving monster.

Telling myself to 'just' eat fewer chocolate-chip cookies didn't help me to break that curious habit. Getting curious about what I *really* wanted and my different options for how to get it was a game changer. The habit SWAP from Pepsi and cookies to belly breathing meditation would never have happened if I said to myself, 'Just eat fewer cookies'. Without getting curious about what I was getting out of the sugar hit (bigger pants and a glucose rollercoaster) and what I wanted (calm), I would never have found the root cause of my bad habit. A full stress bucket and agitation were making me eat cookies. Finding a habit SWAP that addressed agitation as the root cause made the alternative more attractive and allowed change to happen without guilt and blame.

The word 'just' is a red flag that the advice you are giving yourself is wandering into the realm of brutal optimism. If the 'easy solution' that was being offered was actually easy, we would probably be doing it already, and we wouldn't be struggling with the problem. By getting curious and finding the root cause of our habits, we can select another option that allows us to change because we want to, not because we have to.

Brutal optimism is about trying to solve difficult problems with a simplistic solution that doesn't acknowledge the deeper causes of those problems. Easy solutions often fail, and the optimism becomes brutal when people inevitably fail and beat themselves up for it.

Let's get curious

- What things do you find uncomfortable and cause you to resort to toxic positivity for comfort?
- What are your plans to deal with the unhelpful emotions that go along with these?
- How can you dig down and find the root cause?

Chapter 9

Living in the GAP
(I'll be happy when...)

'The way to measure your progress is backward against
where you started, not against your ideal.'
– Dan Sullivan, supercoach

Supercoach Dan Sullivan and organisational psychologist Dr Benjamin
Hardy wrote a brilliant book called *The Gap and the Gain*.

Imagine a continuum charting where you were 10 years ago, where
you are now and the future ideal version of you that you are working
towards (see Figure 9.1, overleaf).

You are always going to be somewhere along that line between
the old you and the ideal version of you. And there's always a gap
between where you are now and your ideal. This gap is usually what
we measure ourselves against – and it's a moving target that always
seems to be out of reach.

What you don't usually see is the distance between the you of
10 years ago and you now – the gain. You don't measure yourself
against your previous self, and therefore you don't experience the
happiness and satisfaction of everything you've achieved in that time.

Sullivan and Hardy say we live too much of our lives in the gap between where we are now and what we think our ideal is, rather than appreciating the gains we've made.

Figure 9.1: The gap and the gain continuum

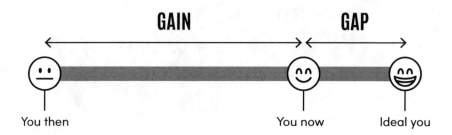

Putting happiness on the other side of the cognitive horizon makes the gap larger. It moves us further away from the better version of ourselves, and in so doing makes us feel more inadequate and unhappy. The bigger the gap, the greater our sense of 'I'm not good enough'. Living in the gap positions you in a place of scarcity and comparison. It makes your self-worth contingent on external validation of your future actions.

Essentialism author Greg McKeown put it this way: **'If you focus on what you lack, you lose what you have. If you focus on what you have, you gain what you lack'**.

People think (and the dictionary even says) that the opposite of scarcity is abundance. What if the opposite of scarcity were simply 'enough'? What if we narrowed the gap by simply being enough, right as we are today? As Dr Brené Brown says, 'abundance and scarcity are two sides of the same coin. The opposite of "never enough" isn't abundance or "more than you could ever imagine". The opposite of scarcity is enough'.

I can hear the overachievers in the room yelling that this kind of thinking will make us apathetic, lazy bastards who won't get off the couch. We need some scarcity for motivation, right?

What if we could still strive from a place of 'enough'? What if we could acknowledge our gains and build on them, but not from a place of 'I'm not good enough'? Would that stop some of the achievers in the world from feeling deeply discontented with their lives, without decreasing their drive to thrive?

Again, it's the difference between 'need' and 'want'. Do you 'need' to have that third Ferrari, or do you 'want' a third Ferrari? We have needs for food, shelter and connection with people we love. I could go on about Maslow and his hierarchy of needs (but I won't), and there is a real difference between them and the things we want. There are a lot of curious habits that stem from wants disguising themselves as needs. Being clear about the difference can move us closer to that ideal version of ourselves and help us build on the gains while shrinking the gap between where we are and where we want to be.

Mind the gap?

You know a story is meant for you when you hear it two or three times in the same week. I'd never heard of Dan Jansen and had no idea who he was, and then his story appeared in an episode of *The Tim Ferriss Show*, a YouTube clip about the Olympics and *The Gap and the Gain*, which I was reading at the time. This was a story that the universe wasn't letting me miss.

Dan could skate. He was fast, but no one knew how fast until the 1984 Winter Olympics. He was only 18 years old and just scraped into the US speed skating team. As a rookie, he wasn't expected to do much, but he ended up finishing fourth – a great result for someone so young. His future looked like it was paved with gold.

By the time Calgary came around in 1988, everyone knew how fast Dan Jansen was. He was the reigning world champion and a hot favourite to win both the 500- and 1000-metre events at the Olympics. Dan considered himself a fast-twitch muscle guy, and the 500-metre was his pet race.

In the early hours of 14 February 1988, Dan was at the Olympic Village and got a call from the hospital back home. His beloved sister Jane had been fighting leukaemia and didn't look like she was going to make it. Dan said goodbye to his sister over the phone. She was too weak to say goodbye back. A few hours later, just before the biggest race of his life, Dan got the news that Jane had passed away.

He decided not to skate. Then his father said, 'What do you think Jane would want you to do?' He thought about it, and he said, 'I think she would want me to skate'. So, without much preparation at all – this was literally minutes before the race – he put his skates on. He was in tears and was trying to mobilise himself to just get through it somehow. But he was completely off-centre emotionally, and just a few feet into the race, he fell. Dan Jansen didn't fall – he just didn't. So, he felt a great sense of failure. Not only did he fail in the race, but he'd also failed Jane – he'd really wanted to do something special for her.

Four days later, he lined up for the 1000-metre and was flying around the track on world-record pace. The stage looked set for a Hollywood ending. Dan was about to win Olympic gold in memory of his sister. There would not be a dry eye in the house. The only problem: Dan fell at the 800-metre mark and lost.

The 1992 Winter Olympics came around. Again, Jansen was the favourite, but again he didn't medal (fourth in the 500-metre and twenty-sixth in the 1000-metre). It looked like Dan Jansen was going to go down in history as the greatest skater *never* to win an Olympic medal.

Dan started working with mindset coach Jim Loehr. They had two mantras: '35.99' and 'I love the 1000'. He wrote both statements in his journal every day and was determined to break the 36-second barrier for the 500-metre race. Thirty-six seconds was to speed skating what the four-minute mile was to Roger Bannister: it hadn't been done and was thought impossible.

Leading up to Lillehammer in 1994, Dan was skating faster than ever. The journalling had paid off. He had broken the 36-second barrier four times in the lead-up and had won another world championship in a world record time of 35.76 seconds. There was never a hotter favourite coming into his 500-metre race at the Olympics. He had to win this time.

Nope!

He stuttered on a corner and came in eighth in the 500-metre. Everyone felt bad for Dan because they knew he was the best speed skater. He'd broken all the records, but he didn't have a single Olympic medal. He was a choker.

Devastated, he spoke to Jim Loehr. They had four days before Dan's final Olympic race, and together he and Jim decided to create a mindset of gratitude. Dan decided to use the race to show the whole world what a gift speed skating had been for him. He wanted to demonstrate the joy he felt being part of the sport, and show gratitude for all the sacrifices people had made to give him the opportunity to do this special thing that he loved so much.

He wasn't going to try to rock the world record in this race. Instead, he wanted to show joy on his face, so people could see how much love he had for the sport, and how grateful he was for the opportunity.

And, lo and behold, Dan Jansen finally won an Olympic gold medal. He broke an Olympic record and stood on the top step at the medal ceremony with a big, grateful smile on his face.

Dan had narrowed the gap. He had detached himself from the result and his recent disappointments and focused on what he'd gained through skating. He'd built on the gains and all his skill and training so that he stood on the starting line with the smallest gap he'd ever had. And he won!

Dan Jansen's story teaches us that the way to narrow the gap is through understanding our past, present and future. To narrow the gap, we need to have **Gratitude, Acceptance and Purpose (GAP)**.

Gratitude

It's easy to write gratitude off as a touchy-feely, warm pile of mush that's nice but doesn't achieve much. However, there is some really cool science showing that gratitude can actually change your physiology.

In our book *Stress Teflon*, my co-author Mick Zeljko and I wanted to help people let stress slide off them. Stress is awesome – it gives you energy and helps you get shit done. The problem is that you can't marinate in it. Stress makes you defensive, and it also makes you dumb. The stress response of fight-or-flight is about being safe, not smart. The smart part of your brain doesn't run the show when you've been fired up and stressing out for too long – it doesn't even get a say. That's when stress starts to stick. We all like to get fired up every now and then, but being too stressed for too long will take the New Brain offline, and can cause burnout.

Gratitude is like a fire hose that brings the flames under control. It fires up the 'calm and disarm' (parasympathetic) nervous system, which decreases stress and gets us out of fight-or-flight mode. Gratitude gets the New Brain back in the game. When it is genuine, it feels good, and your inner sea squirt starts looking for more things to be grateful for.

University of California, Los Angeles neuroscientist Dr Alex Korb describes gratitude as a 'virtuous cycle': the more you do it, the easier it is, and so the more you do it. Gratitude is not a finite resource.

You need more than the absence of a threat to feel grateful, though. You need the safety of a tribe and honest self-awareness to feel truly grateful, and you can't bullshit your way into it. When you have safety, self-awareness and gratitude, they feed each other in an upward spiral.

The health benefits of gratitude are huge. Dr P. Murali Doraiswamy, head of the Division of Biological Psychology at Duke University Medical Center, explained on *ABC News*, 'If [gratitude] were a drug, it would be the world's bestselling product with a health maintenance indication for every major organ system'.

Gratitude helps with health by decreasing your stress responses, but it also helps get you into repair mode. When your body is in a constant state of stress and arousal, the only systems that are turned on are the ones that keep you safe. In fight-or-flight mode, all your biological priorities are about the immediate problems and how to run or box on. They don't give a shit about long-term health.

Say you have a heart valve that's a bit dodgy and needs some repairs. In stress mode, maintenance isn't a priority, so it never gets done. You aren't going to paint the fence if there is a cyclone on its way. In today's society, we seem to always have a cyclone on the way. The fence never gets painted, and the heart valve doesn't get fixed. To get into repair mode and improve our health, things need to swing in the other direction, and gratitude is a great way to do that.

Studies have shown that grateful people are more energetic and less depressed, anxious and lonely. Gratitude makes you more emotionally intelligent, forgiving and creative. Our brain has limited resources; using them for stress, resentment and worry will keep feeding the stress monster.

Looking at the world through a lens of gratitude will calm the farm, connect your two brains and help narrow the gap, because you're focusing on what you have, rather than what you don't have.

Acceptance

Psychologist Carl Rogers said, 'The curious paradox is that when I accept myself just as I am, then I can change'.

Acceptance means acknowledging the tough challenges you have endured, making peace with what happened and ensuring you use your past experiences to learn and grow.

Unpleasant memories and struggles never feel great, and as such, we want to ignore them, distract ourselves or forget them as quickly as we can. The problem with dodging these uncomfortable memories is that we never learn from them. We are destined to repeat them and end up with a huge pile of rubbish under our rug. I believe the universe will keep sending you the same lesson until you learn it. As Winston Churchill famously said, 'Those that fail to learn from history are doomed to repeat it'.

To understand acceptance and its importance in changing habits, it might be a good idea to talk about what acceptance is *not*.

Acceptance is not denial, delusion or rationalisations. You don't have to like, want or be happy about something to accept it. Accepting is also not resigning yourself that things will be like this forever. By accepting something, you are *not* saying that things can't change – but it's not about bullshitting yourself by making up stories with the sole intent of feeling better, either.

Author and leadership expert Annie McCubbin warns people – especially people who are agreeable – of the dangers that can come along with blind acceptance. She explains, 'If you're a bit on the submissive side, or frightened of conflict, the idea of gratitude or acceptance provides a rationale for further submission.' This won't narrow the gap. Annie explains that acceptance can give you a free pass to avoid conflict and accept behaviours that don't help (yours and others'). This isn't the type of acceptance we are after.

Acceptance is a process of understanding where you are. It's like dropping a pin on the Google Maps of your life so you can see where you are and how you got there. But it's not about attaching blame, shame or guilt to your previous decisions or circumstances. It's about seeing where you are in the present moment as a result of your past, and owning it.

It would have been really easy for Dan Jansen to wallow in a pool of self-pity after his run of bad luck and devastating circumstances. The loss of his sister, the failed medal attempts and being labelled a choker would make self-pity an easy default. When you work as hard as Olympians do and fail at the big dance, failure can be hard to accept. Fortunately, Dan had a mindset coach who gave him another option. Jim Loehr had worked with Dan for a few years by the time his last race came about, so he understood the pain and disappointment of the previous failed attempts at Olympic glory. There was no way he was going to let Dan brush them under the rug and pretend they didn't happen.

Acceptance is understanding what got you to this place and getting curious about the options in front of you. When Dan stood on the starting line for his final race, he had options. He could let the memory of past disappointments flood his brain, or he could accept the past and race his last race free from baggage. He chose the second option, and he narrowed the gap.

On 6 May 1968, Neil Armstrong was flying a lunar lander trainer at NASA Headquarters outside Houston. This aircraft was notoriously twitchy and difficult to control. Armstrong had flown it many times, but on this particular day a thruster malfunctioned, and the astronaut had to eject the module before it crashed into the ground in a fiery explosion.

A few hours after the crash, another astronaut, Alan Bean, popped his head into Armstrong's office to say hello. Still in his flight suit, Neil was doing paperwork, and the two astronauts exchanged pleasantries and had a chat. There was no mention of the death-defying incident that had happened earlier.

Down the hall a bit, Bean bumped into a colleague who explained that the lunar lander had malfunctioned and crashed. In shock, he went back to Armstrong's office to make sure he was OK and ask about the crash. Armstrong simply nodded and said, 'Yeah, I lost control and had to bail out of the darn thing'. No stress, no worry, no fuss. Just acceptance. He had been seconds away from death, and his way of dealing with it was to simply learn how to do it better next time and move on.

Theodore Roosevelt has some Stoic-inspired advice that I think can help all of us narrow the gap by increasing our acceptance: **'Do what you can, with what you've got, where you are'**.

There was nothing Dan Jansen or Neil Armstrong could do about the past. Both men learned to accept adversity, learn from it, and move on. You don't have to win speed skating gold medals or land on the moon, but learning the skills of acceptance will certainly narrow the gap.

Purpose

Here's a thought for you to ponder: **You will one day be *dead*. What's the point?**

Inspiring, huh?

If **Gratitude** is mostly about the past and **Acceptance** puts you in the present, **Purpose** looks towards the future. If you look far enough into the future, you won't be alive. Your purpose is about finding useful ways to fill your life between now and when you finally eat the big one and die.

When we talk about purpose, it's really easy to get into self-help mode and talk like an *America's Got Talent* contestant who 'always had a dream' of being the greatest juggling yodeller ever to ride a unicycle, or the YouTuber who is dedicated to building the definitive collection of vintage lawnmowers. If there's something that's super-important to you and you have a 'dream', good luck to you – dig in, juggle away, and mow your vintage socks off. Lifelong dreams are great if you have one and feel passionate about it, but it isn't necessary to have one. If the dream is big enough, by the time you achieve it you'll be nearly dead, just like the dreamless pleb who couldn't give a shit about vintage lawnmowers.

So, what *is* the point? The answer is simple: there isn't one. In a world that's 4.5 billion years old and a universe that's 93 billion light-years across and growing, trust humans to think that the universe has a plan for them. You are a speck of dust on a speck of dust that hangs around for a blink of time. There is no point. (I told you it was going to be inspiring!)

With this in mind, it's easy to get tied up in existential angst and throw your arms up in the air in defeat (that's a curious habit). It's also easy to get all nihilist and not give a shit about anything. You can become like the emo kid whose dyed-black haircut has made his left eye redundant as he spends his days listening to Death Cab for Cutie albums on repeat while waiting for his mum to bring his breakfast down to the basement at two in the afternoon. Nihilism and not giving a shit about anything is no way to live either. We need a purpose, but how do we find one?

Purpose can be a bit like driving at night: your headlights may only illuminate 30 metres in front of you, but you can go a long way with that. You don't need to have a life-changing dream to have a purpose. There is one question that will tell you if you have (at least some) purpose in your life: **Is the world a better place because you are in it?**

If the answer is no, think harder. If it's still no, do something positive and contribute. Help someone, build something, create art, write, mow lawns, yodel while riding a unicycle… whatever, just do something, and do it on purpose. Action gives you answers.

Comedian Tim Minchin is passionately dedicated to the pursuit of short-term goals: solve problems, fix things or help someone. Be micro-ambitious, set an objective that aligns with your identity goals and give it your all. Put your head down and see where your passionate dedication takes you.

Grit author and psychologist Angela Duckworth explains that, 'At its core, the idea of purpose is the idea that what we do matters to people other than ourselves'. I think she and our ginger-headed, piano-playing comedian are on the same page.

Searching for purpose is a curious habit. Your purpose finds you when you start helping other people and contributing to the world.

We talked in chapters 5 and 7 about identity goals and being really clear on the characteristics of the best version of you. Those goals are infinite, intrinsic and intentional. I hope to be 90 years old and still be curious, creative and generous. Along the way, I plan on being passionately dedicated to whatever my headlights are currently illuminating. Your purpose can change; you are not married to one particular purpose – but when you pick one, give it your all while your headlights are on it.

The great thing about combining identity goals and purpose is that your self-worth does not get tied to success or failure. If you turn up as the best version of yourself and that particular venture doesn't go to plan, it's OK. You learn and move on. No harm, no foul. The caveat here is that you have to give it your all. Not giving a shit is a curious habit; we need purpose and we need to care.

Living in the gap is a curious habit that fuels the stress of comparisons and scarcity. Building on past gains while having

Gratitude, Acceptance and Purpose will decrease the gap between you now and the better version of you.

Let's get curious

- What are you grateful for?
- Name three things in your life that would benefit from more acceptance.
- How is the world better because you are in it?

Chapter 10

Compare and despair

'Comparison is the thief of joy.'
– Theodore Roosevelt

Are you tall? Most people will be able to answer that question without much hassle. I'm 6 foot 3 (192 centimetres), so by most people's standards, I'm tall. If I were in the NBA, though, I'd be considered short. Steve Kerr, the little blond point guard who played for the Chicago Bulls in the '90s, was my height, and he looked like a kid out there.

Comparing ourselves with others is hardwired into human DNA. We are a hierarchical species – always have been, always will be. When you meet someone new, there will always be a moment of instant assessment and comparison, even if you're not consciously registering it. We assess physical, social and intellectual differences all the time. But in some cases, comparison can become a curious habit. Its effect on our self-worth is worth getting curious about.

Social comparison theory, first proposed by Leon Festinger in 1954, suggests there is a hardwired, biological instinct that drives us to compare the way we do. Many species have been observed to have the tendency to 'size up competitors'. My friend Dr Bill von Hippel is a professor of evolutionary psychology at the University of Queensland.

He says we (and a lot of other species) look for **objective measures of quality**. A male peacock with a huge plume of feathers sticking out of its butt will be more appealing to a peahen than another peacock with mangy tail feathers that are dull and floppy. Those big feathers make it easier for predators to see him; so, to a horny peahen, the dude strutting around with the big arse feathers must be a quality bird if he can dodge predators with that thing for a tail. He is definitely one worth sharing a nest with.

The problem with social comparison theory in a world with Photoshop and augmented body parts is that finding *objective* measures of quality has become very difficult. On top of that, we don't usually give much thought to what quality actually is. The guy with the sixpack, biceps-on-triceps and the red Ferrari (the human equivalent of the peacock's tail) might be the nicest person in the whole world, or he could just be a pretentious jerk who uses a sports car as a surrogate penis. How can you tell?

The Old Brain gives us the intuitive first crack at summing people up. The problem is that the Old Brain doesn't care about nuance, shades of grey or our priorities. It just makes a quick decision, and the New Brain then goes to work to find evidence that the Old Brain was right. This is why first impressions count and why they are so difficult to change. The New Brain's default is to verify the first impression, *not* to question it. We imagine our logical brain as a judge who weighs up all the options and facts to make a decision. In reality, it's more like a prime minister's press secretary: it *spins* the facts to make the boss look good and confirm the first impression.

The **compare and despair** nature of Western society has got everyone judging themselves against default criteria that they don't like, never chose and don't want. In years gone by (OK boomer), everyone had people in their tribe who were better off than them. They had a better car, bigger house and looked like they were killing it at the game of life. You could see the people who were a few rungs up the ladder from you, and it gave you something to aspire to. Good system.

Social media, influencer culture and unrealistic expectations have put our 'compare and despair' social comparison hardware on steroids. Rather than seeing one or two rungs up the ladder, we have the entire system of social importance in our pockets, all the time. The problem with social comparison is we almost always do it upwards and not down. We live in the gap (as we learned in the previous chapter) and are very aware of what we don't have while taking for granted the gains we have made. If you're constantly reminded of the people who are thinner, younger and richer than you, and have bigger boobs or biceps and bulging social calendars, it's very difficult to maintain the gratitude, acceptance and purpose you need to stop comparing and despairing.

Comparing 100 percent of your life (including toenail fungus, gutters that need cleaning and that nasty ingrown hair that hurts every time you sit down) with the filtered, edited and curated top-one-percent version of some Insta-glamorous person's life is a recipe for disaster. It's like trying to compare the burger in the menu picture with the one that arrives on your table: it never looks as good, and no matter how delicious it tastes, you feel cheated. Social media leads us to believe everyone is having the perfect time while our life looks like a flat, boring cheeseburger. No wonder we are despairing.

Apples with apples

There is a website called ratemyagent.com.au that real estate agents use to see where they sit in the pecking order of sales in their target neighbourhoods. It ranks them in order of sales and tells them who sells what percentage of the market they are selling in. This type of data can be motivating – if you're an up-and-coming agent, seeing yourself move up a place or two can really fire you up. If you have a poor run, though, chances are 'compare and despair' will kick in, opening the door to imposter syndrome. Your confidence will take a dive – not ideal in real-estate land.

My friend Connor is in his twenties, and he and his brother have taken over the family agency. He is killing it by taking advantage of new technology and adding some spice and fun to the marketing process. I was talking to the brothers, and Connor told me about ratemyagent. com.au and that he was really proud that he had risen to number eight in the neighbourhood lately. 'I thought you'd be higher', I said, having noticed the number of sales he had made in the last few months.

His brother, Tiger, chimed in and pointed out that the other agents had been established a lot longer and they had to chip away to move up. He then said something profound: 'You can't compare your story at chapter 3 with someone else who is at chapter 10'.

His words – so wise for such a young person – show the importance of understanding where you're at in your journey. Comparing is a curious habit that needs context to be helpful. Having something to aspire to and goals to aim for are essential for growth, but you need to get curious when you start comparing apples with oranges.

Lost connections

In his book *Lost Connections*, journalist Johann Hari takes a deep dive into depression and anxiety. He looks at why we are getting sadder even though the world is getting safer and we *appear* more connected than at any time in history. Hari struggled with depression and anxiety for most of his life and spent nearly two decades on medication to try and help with his mental health. He spoke to experts from all over the world in his quest to better understand depression and anxiety. As the title of the book suggests, he found one common denominator: lost connections. He explored our connections to nature, connections to purpose and, most of all, connections to people. He had an epiphany when he wondered: **'What if depression is, in fact, a form of grief – for our own lives not being as they should?'**

What if the despair we feel when we compare ourselves to others is actually grief for the in-person connections we have lost, yet still need?

Hari is quick to point out that social media platforms have their good points. They create connections, and that is very important. The problem is, they don't create the strong personal connections that make us feel entrenched in our tribe. He explained virtual versus in-person connections as a 'bit like the difference between pornography and sex: it addresses a basic itch, but it's never satisfying'.

Hari describes depression and anxiety as a normal reaction to an environment that is no longer lining up with our biology. It is normal to compare and rate ourselves against other people. What *isn't* normal is the imbalance in our comparisons. We are not comparing apples with apples, and our envy for other people's manicured and curated highlight reels is fuelling the curious habit of comparing and despairing.

In a 2015 study, Dr Ethan Kross found that 'the more time people spent passively scrolling through Facebook, peering in on the lives of others, the more envy they experienced and the worse they subsequently felt'.

When the number of likes, shares and retweets you receive becomes a measure of your self-worth, things have got to change. There is a social media platform for just about every type of comparison you can think of:

- Facebook: How busy and exciting your life is
- Instagram: How pretty you and your life are
- Twitter: How clever and witty you are
- Snapchat: How many of your friends can you distract with emojis?
- LinkedIn: How successful and important you are
- Pinterest: How good do my throw cushions look?

It didn't start off that way. In 2002, Mike Krieger was a student at Stanford and managed to get into a class in B.J. Fogg's Persuasive Technologies Lab. (Remember, Fogg was the dude who put sunshine into the habit loop.) In this course, they learned all about B.F. Skinner, habit loops, reward-based learning and behaviour change.

For one assignment, Mike was paired up with a likeable computer nerd called Tristan Harris who loved coding and doing magic. They were asked to build an app that would influence people's behaviour. Tristan had become curious about a psychological phenomenon called 'seasonal affective disorder' (SAD). If you have ever lived in a cold climate, you will have some idea of SAD. The short days in winter have a very real effect on people's mood.

Having lived in England for a number of years, I can attest to the miserable effects of SAD during the dark, gloomy days of winter. English people have a reputation for being rigid, dour and stiff. That was never my experience; many Brits I encountered had a sharp wit and were great fun. By the time February came around, though, even the most upbeat of them were starting to be more like Margaret Thatcher than Michael McIntyre. They became temporarily miserable. Only when the trees started greening up and the days got longer did people (me included) start smiling again. By spring I could wander back into Luke-land and enjoy the sun, complete with unicorns farting rainbows.

Mike and Tristan decided to build an app to try and help people with SAD. The theory: link people on opposite sides of the world and 'send the sunshine'. The app would track online weather reports for both people's locations, and when one person had a string of shitty days, it would prompt the other to send them some sunshine. What a lovely idea. It showed people that someone cared about them and helped lift the spirits of friends who might be struggling with seasonal depression.

A few years after building *Send the Sunshine*, Mike teamed up with Kevin Systrom, another student from B.J.'s course, and they started looking into the joy people get from sharing photos online. Facebook was exploding at this point, and Mike and Kevin knew the power of immediate rewards, likes and pretty little love hearts. They knew that people love dopamine hits and feeling like they're part of a tribe. In 2012, they used this knowledge to build an app.

The app was Instagram, and just two years later, they sold it to Facebook for US$1 billion. That was huge back then, but it would soon be dwarfed by the US$19 billion that Facebook paid for WhatsApp just two years later. Social media is big business. Likes, shares, follows and retweets have tapped into the dopamine reward centres of a generation.

In 2022, it is estimated that Instagram has approximately 1.4 billion users and is now worth US$109 billion. It accounts for about a third of parent company Meta's advertising revenue. The light of social media is burning brightly for the masses. If you ever stop at a traffic light at night and look at the car next to you, the driver's crutch will often be softly lit up by a mysterious blue glow. If that driver is under 30, chances are Instagram is open in their lap. Social media is about connection, and that is something we desperately desire and need.

The Insta tribe

One of the foundational concepts in my book *Stress Teflon* is the **safety of the tribe**. As humans, we need people we love and who love us. To prehistoric people, being alone was a death sentence. The main reason humans have survived as long as we have is our ability to work together. There is a whole cocktail of chemicals designed to motivate our inner sea squirt to connect with others. Serotonin, dopamine and oxytocin make it pleasurable to feel part of a tribe and to be loved.

Stress hormones adrenaline and cortisol get released when you are alone to motivate you to get off your bum and find some friends.

Imagine you have had a bad day at work and feel stressed. You are marinating in cortisol; it is pumping around your body, making you feel twitchy and uncomfortable. Stress hormones bias you towards action. Your brain goes in search of something to make you feel better. The last time you posted a picture on Facebook, a bunch of people liked it. That felt good; let's do that again. You find a photo, edit it, throw it through a filter or two and send it out into cyber-land. You still hate your job, and your cat is eyeing the can of tuna you are eating for dinner. Fortunately, your photo from last year's holiday looks great and all your friends are liking the crap out of it. The instant gratification of cyber validation gives you a little dopamine hit to make you feel better, without actually doing anything to change your circumstances.

Social media helps people feel they are part of a tribe. 'If it isn't on Instagram, it didn't happen' is a modern-day version of 'If a tree falls in the forest and nobody is there to hear it, does it make a sound?' It provides a vehicle for people to show that they care and keeps people communicating. Should be a good system, right?

Like a lot of curious habits, social media is useful until it isn't. If we go back to our definitions of addiction in chapter 1 – 'a progressive narrowing of things that bring you pleasure' and 'continuing use despite adverse consequences' – social media ticks both boxes.

When social media changes from a tool for connection to a *need* for validation, it becomes a curious habit. It narrows the things that bring us joy, and we continue to use it despite adverse consequences.

Rather than being in the moment, some people are obsessed with capturing the moment, filtering the moment, and editing and sharing the moment. Would it not be better to simply *be* in the moment?

Social media isn't the only thing that causes us to compare and despair, but it has hacked into our Old Brain wiring and created one hell of a curious habit. It's good, until it isn't.

Let's get curious

- What default habit loops do you have with social media?
- Is social media connection or validation to you?
- How can you use social media more deliberately?

Chapter 11

Hey look, something shiny!

'Every great waste of time begins with a small distraction.'
– Anonymous

Our brains are designed to make us pay attention to things that are out of the ordinary. Noticing movement in a bush thousands of years ago could have been the difference between hunting and gathering your lunch and becoming something else's lunch. We get bigger dopamine hits for rewards that are unexpected, and our brains start looking for those rewards more often. Think of how great it feels when you find $50 in the jacket that you haven't worn since last winter.

Why, then, has distraction become such a curious habit? My wife claims that I am like a squirrel: 'Hey look, something shiny!' I think she may have a point. Keeping focused on one thing is getting harder for me these days, and I suspect I'm not alone.

Technology has put 'shiny' things everywhere, especially when it comes to our phones. The buzz of a text, the ping of email and little hearts that pop up on Facebook are all shiny things that demand our attention.

So, your phone pings, and you see somebody has tagged you in a photo. What happens? First, you get a burst of dopamine in the reward pathway in the brain. That feels good. Curiosity gets the better of you and you open up Facebook. It may be a long-lost photo that you haven't seen in years (the joy of nostalgia), or it may be a photo of your mate Joanne's avocado toast (she knows you like a good smashed avo). Who knows what little surprise that ping is alerting you to? The possibility of it being something good is like a little dopamine lollipop, and everybody loves a lollipop. Your inner sea squirt wants less of the discomfort of the unknown and more of the possible good stuff. Where's my phone?

Once this has happened 10, 20, 50 or even 100 times, it's not as exciting as it was the first time. That's the brain changing in response to that pleasurable experience. Things that used to be pleasurable lose their allure when they get repeated too often. Psychologists call this 'hedonic adaptation'. Even things you really like become less appealing and give you smaller dopamine lollipops when they're repeated. You may love lobster, but if you ate it every day at every meal, it would get old pretty quick.

That's where technology does its sneaky little mind trick! Unpredictable rewards keep your inner sea squirt guessing, so the brain doesn't become used to the pleasure. Social media mixes up the rewards, dangling a curiosity carrot in front of you, and keeps you interested by doing so. It uses curiosity to cause discomfort and sucks you into looking more closely, distracting you from more important things.

As I mentioned in chapter 2, every morning I spend an hour on my exercise bike reading my Kindle. This is when I do my best learning. Doing it early helps, because to learn something, you need to focus, and that requires fewer distractions. A few weeks ago, I was reading a book, had music in my headphones and was getting a bunch of texts from mates with surf reports. I checked my email three times and booked some tickets to a concert that just got announced. This was during the time I had designated for exercise and learning. I just happened to be reading *Indistractable: How to Control Your Attention and Choose Your Life*, by Nir Eyal, and the irony wasn't lost on me.

As a behaviour designer, Nir Eyal has an interesting take on distraction. He's another B.J. Fogg prodigy and has written two books that look at distraction from completely different angles. His first book, *Hooked*, was a how-to guide for building products that get people hooked (think social media, online gambling and Pokémon GO). Ironically, *Indistractable*, his second book, is about how to resist these products and function in a world that is full of shiny things.

According to Nir Eyal, 'Big Tech' is about getting, using and selling people's attention. If you can get people's attention, you can trigger cravings that build desire and eventually separate people from their hard-earned cash. As we discovered in the last chapter, social media is big business. Unfortunately, the product they are selling is our attention.

Eyal defines a distraction as anything that takes you away from something you planned to do. Traction is anything you do with intent that gives you forward motion in the desired direction. So, distraction is the opposite of traction: it stops you from doing things with intent.

He says: **'Traction moves you towards what you really want while distraction moves you further away. Being indistractable means striving to do what you say you will do'.**

If we define traction as 'moving towards something we really want', it makes me wonder if perhaps distraction is made worse by not being clear on exactly what we want. Remember the wise words from the Stoic philosopher Seneca: 'If you don't know which port you are heading for, no wind is favourable'.

My morning routine of riding and reading is the favourite part of my day. It's a bit like Admiral William H. McRaven's famous 'make your bed' habit: 'If you make your bed every morning you will have accomplished the first task of the day'. If I do some exercise and learn something early in my day, I have achieved *something*, no matter how the rest of my day pans out. This hour is a precious gift I give myself every morning, and letting distractions detract from it was not doing me any favours.

Like a lot of curious habits, distractions aren't inherently bad. Quite often, the real joys in life come from the shiny things out to the side. Putting the blinkers on and permanently blocking out everything in the periphery is a sure-fire way to miss out on a big chunk of life's joy. To be 'indistractable' doesn't mean never looking for the shiny things in your periphery – rather, it simply means that you need to do it deliberately. Check your email, scroll Instagram or look at videos of dogs on skateboards if that floats your boat. The trick, according to Nir, is to do it on purpose and designate time to do it without losing traction.

Eyal loves social media, but he uses it purposefully. He doesn't let internal triggers of boredom, stress or anxiety send him down an infinite-scrolling rabbit hole. If he's going to look at socials, he allocates time to do it and keeps making traction towards his goals.

Technology, and social media in particular, has become an adult version of a baby's dummy. Whenever we feel bored, anxious, sad or agitated, social media becomes a way to calm the farm. Unfortunately, research is showing that excessive reliance on technology is creating 'noise', making our attention spans shrink while increasing our stress levels. Shawn Achor defines 'noise' as anything that creates distractions without adding any benefit. Social media, the news, unwanted emails and cold calls are all examples of noise. I think we can expand the definition of 'noise' to include anything that gets in the way of your good habits or causes you to make non-productive decisions about where to send your attention.

A group of young tech industry leaders started to get disillusioned with the effect of their inventions and banded together to reverse the damage they had caused. Remember Mike Krieger and Tristan Harris, who designed the app *Send the Sunshine*? Both men understood B.J. Fogg's strategies and could design technology to hook people and keep them engaged.

As a kid, Tristan had been an amateur magician. He knew how to distract attention while he performed his tricks using sleight of hand. He spent his summers at magic camp, and over the years he learned from some of the best magicians around. Magic, he was told, was all about exploiting weaknesses in people's attention. The nerdy trips to magic camp would come in very handy for Tristan as, with the help of B.J. Fogg, he learned to do magic by exploiting human frailties and using the 'reinforcements' that B.F. Skinner had discovered six decades before.

Tristan developed an app that allowed you to click on a word and have a pop-up appear that told you the basics about that topic without having to open a new window and fall down the rabbit holes that go along with that. Google wanted Tristan's technology and threw bucketloads of cash at him to incorporate it into their Chrome browser. Google bought Tristan's company and gave him a job at Google headquarters. As he rode up Silicon Valley's ladder of importance, though, something was beginning to gnaw at his conscience, and he began to wonder about the ethics of what they were doing.

As I mentioned earlier, B.J. Fogg and his graduates were changing the face of Silicon Valley. Fogg tried to instil the same lesson as Peter Parker's (aka Spider-Man's) uncle, who said, 'With great power comes great responsibility'. His course always included ethical debates, as he drilled into his students the importance of using their skills to make the world *better*.

As the years went on and technology got more sophisticated, companies like Google, Facebook and Apple gained the ability to build detailed psychological profiles on their customers and target them with information or advertising that they knew would push their buttons. This was the beginning of what Harvard professor Shoshana Zuboff would come to call 'surveillance capitalism'. Big Tech was making money by studying you and your habits and selling that information to companies that wanted your business. If they had to distract you to get you to engage, that's whated they would do. Fogg's lessons on ethics didn't stick quite as well as he'd hoped.

The old saying that principles are only tested when there's money involved rings true. The magic lessons Fogg taught about triggers and changing habits were being put to use to rob us of our ability to focus. Tristan and his friends decided to push back.

Google's mission is 'to organize the world's information and make it universally accessible and useful'. It doesn't mention who it's useful to and who gets access to what information.

Tristan started voicing concerns about the effect their products were having on people and their concentration. Colleagues started to take notice of what he was saying, and so Google created a new role for him: he became Google's first 'design ethicist', and it was his job to make sure Google's products didn't do (as much) harm.

A few frustrating years later, Tristan left Google. It seemed that designing ethical technology that helped people maintain their focus didn't sit well when it made the company less money. It must have felt a bit like the scene in *Jerry Maguire* where Tom Cruise proposes to do a better job but make the company less money. At the big end of tech town, this goes down like pork sausages at a vegan buffet in a synagogue.

Tristan Harris went on to testify in front of a US Senate inquiry about Big Tech, and also produced the Netflix documentary *The Social*

Dilemma. His mission is to try and help people wrestle their focus back from their technology and decrease the effect of surveillance capitalism.

The curious habit of constant distraction is a tough one to reverse. As Tristan points out in his documentary, it didn't start out with sinister intentions. Social media simply evolved, and like most businesses, social media companies doubled down on the areas that were the most profitable. Selling your information, wants and desires has made Google, Facebook and Microsoft the biggest companies in the world.

Without getting into a big conspiracy theory, these social media companies' algorithms are improving all the time, and the more information the AI gets, the better it gets at working out where you are likely to spend your money. It then sells your info to those companies you are likely to buy from. This provides the basis for surveillance capitalism, and the scary thing is that the algorithms they have now are nothing compared to what's coming. It's like mums in 1981 worrying about *Space Invaders* without any clue about how good (and addictive) *Fortnite* was going to get.

So, what can we do to save our attention and stop noise and distractions?

Noise-cancelling habits

Airline travel can be stressful. There are strict timetables, gate changes and people who don't understand the concept of 'no liquids' holding up the line at security. One thing that significantly decreases the stress of flying is noise-cancelling headphones. I put them on at take-off and the sound of the engine disappears, along with the snoring from the businessman hogging the armrest next to me. By wearing noise-cancelling headphones, I instantly get rid of numerous distractions.

The one habit – putting on the noise-cancelling headphones – eliminates five or six other distractions.

One of the most useful things you can do to prevent distraction is to identify your sources of noise and eliminate them. Say one of the habits that you are trying to foster is to get more sleep. Everything from food to light to actual noise can make a good sleep more difficult. One of the best things that you can do to improve sleep is install block-out curtains. A dark room definitely improves sleep. Installing block-out curtains is a noise-cancelling intervention that you only need to do once, and it has a beneficial effect forever.

As we've discussed, phones are a massive distraction and also our biggest generator of attention-stealing 'noise'. Every buzz, ding and notification becomes a distraction, and studies have shown it can take up to 20 minutes to get back into the flow you had before the distraction. There are heaps of noise-cancelling habits we can introduce with regards to our phones. I'm sure you can think of several. I'm going to give you two:

1. **Turn off notifications:** No more ping, no more buzz and no more little red circles to pop up and challenge your attention. As far as noise-cancelling habits go, this one has the greatest bang for your buck. It takes 11 seconds and eliminates hundreds of distractions forever. Removing these distractions also decreases the dopamine addiction that is creating a generation of people who are turning into life-support systems for their iPhones.

2. **Charge your phone in another room:** Time spent connecting with loved ones is precious. No one ever lay on their deathbed wishing they'd spent more time on Instagram. Yet we are often so distracted by our phones that conversations are stilted, and the time spent with family and friends becomes less special. I have a noise-cancelling habit of charging my phone in my home office (near the entrance to the house). I keep the sound on and can

hear phone calls, but I'm not distracted or continually fighting the urge to grab my phone. My friends know to ring if they need me, and I will check email and texts when I want to check them. One habit eliminates the need to make hundreds of distracting decisions. The other benefit of charging your phone in another room is that the phone isn't next to your bed.

If some is good, more must be better, right?

I have an issue with moderation. Having had a 'some is good, more is better' mindset my entire life, I've always had a minor weight problem. I needed to lose 10 to 15 kilograms for about 20 years. Three years ago, I discovered the joys of intermittent fasting. How many food-related decisions do you estimate you make every day? Most people say around 15. When scientists measured this, though, they found the number to be more than 200.

Good to Great author and leadership guru Jim Collins said, 'Look for single decisions that remove hundreds or thousands of other decisions'. Intermittent fasting is one decision that eliminates more than 200 others. While doing a fast, all my food-related choices are off the table. With less noise, you get more brainpower to dedicate to other things. Thanks to the noise-cancelling benefits of fasting, I lost the 15 kilograms and have kept it off for the last three years. No more stress of yo-yo diets.

There is an old adage that 100 percent committed is easier than 99 percent. It may only be 1 percent, but that tiny seed of doubt, friction and indecision can derail things in ways that defy the maths. When you start fasting, it's tough – you have to do the grunt work to SWAP your habits and defy your inner sea squirt. But eventually, your body and brain get used to it, and it's a relief to shave 199 decisions off your mental load.

Turning off notifications, putting your phone in the next room, and deciding to have a 'fast day' are all examples of noise-cancelling habits. As Michael Jordan famously said: **'Once I made a decision, I never thought about it again'**.

Let's get curious

- What settings on your phone will you change to decrease 'noise'?
- Where are you going to charge your phone from now on?
- What are three noise-cancelling habits you are going to try?

Chapter 12

All by myself: pulling away

'The fact that you're struggling doesn't make you a burden.
It doesn't make you unlovable or undesirable or
undeserving of care. It doesn't make you too much or
too sensitive or too needy. It makes you human.'
– Daniell Koepke

David Lloyd is a big unit. He loves the gym, has a bunch of cool tattoos and can bench press a small truck. It would have made a big thump when he hit the ground after falling six metres off the roof where he was fitting solar panels. He may be tough, but the concrete won that particular battle. A mangled left leg, broken right ankle, shattered left wrist and a bunch of broken ribs were all proof that concrete is harder than humans. David was messed up. He had several operations on his shattered legs, and the physios worked him over pretty hard while he was in the hospital. He knew that with a bit of determination, his broken body would heal.

David had plenty of determination. What the big fella didn't realise was the effect an accident like this would have on his mind. He was

OK in hospital – he chatted to the nurses and accepted the painful challenges from the physios and the occupational therapists. His body was hurting, but mentally he was alright. The emotional challenges revealed themselves when he got home. He began to struggle with the mental demons of having his identity taken away.

We have talked a lot in this book about creating your identity deliberately – building habits that correspond to the type of person you want to be. In your twenties, as David is, a lot of your identity is linked to what you do. David is a tradie (an electrician) and loved the gym, cycling, kicking the footy and having a few beers with his mates – regular Aussie bloke stuff. Even the Sunday bushwalks with his fiancée Laura were out, and the identity he wanted was ripped away from him.

The accident took away a lot of the things that brought David joy and made him who he was. Friends popped around a lot at the start, but the visits decreased quickly in both quantity and quality. David was miserable. A deep depression had settled in, and he found himself pulling away from the people he loved, even Laura. At his rock bottom, David was considering suicide as an option.

David went back to work too quickly and couldn't do a lot of the physical stuff he'd done before. Pushing harder just gave him more pain and stalled his recovery. He felt useless. He thought he was a burden, and he just wanted to crawl into a hole and stay there. His mental health was in the toilet.

As he started to gain more mobility, though, his mental health improved slightly, and he had an epiphany: lots of people must feel like this. In the hospital, you get lots of support. Once you go home, that support dries up, and it's easy to start pushing it away. Around this time, David joined one of my programs, called Prymal Reset. We did an audit of his thought habits, particularly around guilt and shame. He was feeling like a burden to everyone, especially Laura.

He was withdrawing from his tribe because he didn't want to be a liability. He felt ashamed.

Dr Brené Brown has a great way of differentiating between shame and guilt that I think can help all of us. The way she puts it, 'guilt is I've *done* something bad, shame is I *am* something bad'. Dr Brown's research found that when you are marinating in shame, you are much more likely to struggle with drugs, alcohol, excessive eating, depression and anxiety. Guilt, on the other hand, sparks curiosity. You learn the lessons, improve and grow. Guilt is the teacher that tells you what not to do next time.

David was in a shame shitstorm. He had always been fiercely independent, and having to rely on other people didn't sit comfortably with him. His thought habit loops all led to his inner sea squirt telling him to pull away and not be a burden. The sadder he got, the more he shut people out.

When David looks back on that time, he remembers feeling the most shame when he saw his dad: 'I felt so guilty when I saw my dad, like I was letting him down, and I resented myself for it'. David was chewing on a shame sandwich because his dad had taken three months off work to be with him. He just hated himself for putting his dad out, even though any parent would do the same for their kid. He knew he would do the same if he had a kid in the same boat.

It's a curious habit in modern society, particularly in the West, that depression makes us withdraw from the one thing that could fix our depression: our tribe. Depression thrives when we close ourselves off from connection. There's a curious thing going on with a generous person like David: he loves helping people; it gives him joy to help someone out. Why wouldn't he let others get the same joy by helping him? His shame was digging a pit of isolation that was getting deeper every day.

Pulling away when you need people the most is a curious habit. The anxiety triggered by feelings of embarrassment or shame feels bad. Your inner sea squirt pulls away from that feeling. The result: depression and isolation. Anxiety is designed to make you move – it's there to help you get to safety or to tribe up. Anxiety should help you seek people who make you feel safe and who have your back. But does it? Maybe not. For a lot of people, anxiety makes them withdraw, feel awkward and pull away.

We think of anxiety and depression as being different things. In his book *Lost Connections*, Johann Hari concludes that you can't separate the two. The National Institutes of Health – the main body funding medical research in the USA – has stopped funding studies that depict depression and anxiety as different diagnoses. One in five adults in the USA is taking medication for a psychiatric problem, and depression and anxiety are the main culprits.

Hari describes depression and anxiety as being cover versions of the same song. Depression is the downbeat version played by the emo band with dyed black hair and pasty skin. Anxiety is the same song being sung by a screaming thrash metal band. They have the same sheet music, but it sounds different. One thing for certain is that both anxiety and depression improve when you have the safety of a tribe.

Getting curious about why you are pulling away can lead to a deliberate habit loop of asking for and accepting help. Showing gratitude, connecting and paying it forward create an upward spiral that connects us all and helps everyone stop the downward dive into isolation and depression.

As for David, he decided to *do* something. He started Two Feet Foundation to help people get over trauma and connect with people who have been through similar issues. He launched a podcast and is helping local hospitals to start Two Feet support groups to connect people and help their mental health. Action gives you answers, and doing something was the way that the big fella got out of his hole and is helping others do the same.

Pulling away from your tribe when you feel down is a curious habit. You need the safety of a tribe, and having the self-awareness to catch yourself pulling away in the tough times can be a cue to get curious and connect.

Let's get curious

- Who will you connect with if you start feeling down or sad?
- When does shame creep into your world?
- How is the world (and your tribe) better because you're in it?

Chapter 13

Fear of being scared

'We were scared, but our fear was not
as strong as our courage.'
– Malala Yousafzai

Nearly 100 years ago, a young lady called Claire Weekes was on track
to become the first female to be awarded a Doctor of Science by the
University of Sydney. It was 1927 and the soon-to-be Dr Weekes
developed inflammation of her tonsils, lost weight and started having
heart palpitations. Tuberculosis was a big threat of the day. With
scant evidence, a doctor diagnosed her with TB and sent her off to a
sanitarium outside the city.

Scared, alone and ruminating about the thought of imminent
death, Claire spent six months in the sanitarium and emerged in a
worse state than when she went in. She was anxious and struggling
with what we would now call 'panic attacks' (they didn't have words
for it then). She called it 'nervous illness'.

Claire got talking to a friend who had returned from World War I.
He told her about the men who had suffered from shellshock after the
war and gave her some life-changing advice on what he had learnt
from them. He explained that soldiers had been programmed by fear,

and in doing so they were getting the same physical signs that she was, even off the battlefield: the racing heartbeat, the sweaty palms and ruminating about imminent peril. Claire's scientific curiosity took over. She questioned her soldier friend about how best to deal with the problem. His advice would help her get through this harrowing time and give her the tools to deal with fear and anxiety.

So, what was his lesson? **'Lean into fear!'**

The soldier explained, 'Don't fight the fear, let it float by'. For Claire, this was a revelation. She took the advice, added to it and created a system for dealing with fear and anxiety. Her system included a six-word mantra: **'Face, accept, float, let time pass'**.

Using this mantra, she learned how to recognise the first sign of feeling anxious (face), accept that these were uncomfortable feelings, and let the feelings float on by like a cloud in the sky. By doing this, she recovered quite quickly, and her 'nervous illness' became something she learned to live with, and not something to fear.

Our curious fear of fear

In the early 2000s, Aussie rock band Something for Kate reminded us that we aren't the first to think that everything has already been thought before. But long before we had terms like PTSD, ADHD and OCD, people like Claire Weekes were getting curious about fear, anxiety and why we do the things we do. Dr Weekes wasn't the first to work out the difference between a reaction and a response, though. Once again, Viktor Frankl, Holocaust survivor and author of *Man's Search for Meaning*, summed it up beautifully: **'The one thing you can't take away from me is the way I choose to respond to what you do to me. The last of one's freedoms is to choose one's attitude in any given circumstance'**.

A couple of thousand years before all this new-fangled psycho-babble was invented, the Romans and Greeks had worked a lot of this stuff out. Seneca wrote: **'We suffer more from imagination than from reality'**. And there is an old Swedish proverb that states: **'Worry often gives a small thing a big shadow'**.

See what I'm getting at? The fear of being scared is a curious habit that has been around for a long time.

Self-help for your nerves

Fast-forward 40 years and Dr Claire Weekes had enjoyed a stellar career in science, in which she'd forged a new understanding about evolutionary biology, particularly in reptiles. She studied medicine and went on to become a general practitioner (GP) who gained a reputation for helping patients with 'nervous illness'.

The lessons she learned in her twenties from a returned soldier, and her understanding of how our evolutionary systems work, became the basis of her medical practice. In 1962, at the age of 59, she published the first of five books: the global bestseller *Self-Help for Your Nerves*. In the book, she was critical of both the Freudian psycho-analysis approach (lie on the couch and talk about sex and childhood) and the behaviourists (Thorndike and Skinner, who we met earlier in this book). To her, these approaches weren't helpful because they were all about masking fear, rather than facing and accepting reality.

By the 1970s she had refined her theories even more. She wrote: **'The nervous person must understand that when he panics, he feels not one fear, as he supposes, but two separate fears. I call these the first and second fear'**. (She was good at science, but her marketing was a bit Marie Kondo.)

The first fear, Claire said, is the biological part of our 'fight, flight and freeze' reaction, and there is nothing we can do about it.

The second fear is a response to the first, and it is here where we have a choice. For a lot of people, the default habit loop is to push back, fight the fear response or try to distract themselves – 100 percent sea squirt mode. 'This feels bad, let's move away from it.'

Dr Weekes figured out all those years ago that 100 percent sea squirt mode works until it doesn't. She concluded that her patients did not necessarily suffer from 'nervous illness' because they had flawed personalities or traumatic childhoods. Rather, the problems were caused by the patient having a habit of dodging fear (fear avoidance), made worse or caused by a very responsive 'sensitised' nervous system that was in the habit of being on edge all the time.

One way to decrease the second type of fear is to get comfortable with the first. In the 1980s, Susan Jeffers wrote a book called *Feel the Fear and Do It Anyway*, and that one sentence is great advice for dealing with the second fear. Worrying about worry is a curious habit that we do have control over.

Deep into her eighties, Dr Weekes was asked in an interview if she'd ever had panic disorder. She replied, 'Yes, I have had what you call panic attacks. In fact, I still have them. Sometimes they wake me at night'. Her interviewer told her he was sorry to hear that. Dr Weekes looked at him in shock, and she responded: **'Save your sympathy for someone else. I don't need it or want it. What you call a panic attack is merely a few normal chemicals that are temporarily out of place in my brain. It is of no significance whatsoever to me!'**

Let's get curious

- What physical responses do you have when you worry?
- What does 'leaning into fear' look like to you?
- Where in your life are you dodging fear?

Chapter 14

The doctor will fix me

'When a flower doesn't bloom, you fix the environment in
which it grows, not the flower.'
– Alexander den Heijer

Dr Weekes understood decades ago that feeling anxious doesn't mean
there is anything wrong with you. Anxiety, sadness, fear and worry
are often perfectly logical and understandable responses to life in a
complex world. In recent years, we (society and the medical profession)
have started a curious habit of 'medicalising' normal physical and
mental responses. Feeling anxious has turned into 'generalised anxiety
disorder' (GAD). Kids not wanting to sit still and concentrate has
become 'attention deficit hyperactivity disorder' (ADHD). Any sign of
prolonged sadness gets you diagnosed with depression. I'm not saying
these conditions don't exist; they most certainly do. The problem,
I think, lies with our well-meaning doctors, who have a curious habit
of convincing us there's something wrong with us and pumping us full
of Valium, Adderall and Prozac.

I once went to the GP for a yearly check-up and happened to
mention that I was feeling 'a bit flat'. My business was pumping, my
wife and daughter were well, and I was still doing all the fun things

I usually do. I had been running busy optometry businesses for over 20 years by this stage. Testing eyes all day, I had asked, 'Which one is clearer: number one or number two?' over 9.5 million times. I was definitely living in sea squirt mode, bored and stuck in the path of least resistance. I was phoning it in and had lost the CARE factor (more on this in chapter 20) and some of the passion for the business of testing eyes. No wonder I was 'a bit flat'.

I wasn't consciously aware of any of this at the time – success can hide a multitude of troubles. I just wasn't quite my usual excitable self. The three minutes of uninsightful questions from the GP uncovered nothing. 'Let's try this and see how you go', said the doc as my 12 minutes came to a close. I left with a prescription for Lexapro, an antidepressant that would help elevate my serotonin levels.

Serotonin is our 'pride from inside' hormone – the one that tells your body you are safe, you are secure and you are 'enough'. Selective serotonin reuptake inhibitors (SSRIs) like what I was prescribed have helped people, but many experts believe they are nowhere near as good as the drug companies make out and the doctors would hope. According to the Australian Bureau of Statistics, 1.7 million (7.8 percent of) Australians take antidepressants. Most of these drugs arguably have *relatively* few side effects, and this makes prescribing them less risky for the doctors who, to their credit, are trying to help. Unfortunately, good intentions don't ensure the drugs do much good. The road to placebo-town is paved with good intentions.

Johann Hari's book *Lost Connections* is about finding hope for people with anxiety and depression. He and the scientists he interviewed challenge the assumption that depression and anxiety are chemical imbalances arising from faulty neurochemistry. He quotes Professor Andrew Scull of Princeton University, who explained that attributing depression to low serotonin is 'deeply misleading and unscientific'.

Professor Joanna Moncrieff is an expert in brain chemistry at University College London. Her take is that there's no evidence of a chemical imbalance causing the problems of anxiety and depression. She went on to explain that the scientific world wouldn't know what a chemically balanced brain would look like, anyway. In her book *The Myth of a Chemical Cure*, she scoffs at the idea of mental distress being caused by brain chemicals that are out of balance.

The chemicals in your brain are a response to what's going on in your world and how you are viewing it. The idea that you can leave your world the same and just fix the chemicals is a myth sold to us by the pharmaceutical industry. It's like having a dying pot plant that's been stuck in a dark corner with pot-bound roots, crap soil and no light. You can squirt Miracle-Gro on it all day long and it won't get better. You have to change its environment. Chop off the dead leaves and give it a bigger pot, some fresh soil and a bit of light, and the plant will have a fighting chance.

Drug companies are making a fortune from medications for depressed people, and these same companies fund the research into their effectiveness. Any study that casts a shadow on their drug's efficiency will get buried quicker than a snitch in a mob film. It is a bit like KFC advertising the results of a study on the effectiveness of Zinger burgers as a weight-loss tool. More than 40 percent of all studies commissioned by drug companies are never published, and the scientists who perform them are under enormous pressure to get the desired result. There are people way more qualified than me to talk about the morality of Big Pharma, but using chemicals as the first port of call for mental health problems is something we need to get curious about.

Being given antidepressants was my cue to get curious. As someone who lives in Luke-land – a place where unicorns fart rainbows, everyone is nice and everything always works out – the idea of being depressed was not something I could accept without challenge. I decided to look into serotonin and what it does. It turns out, a spritz of serotonin brings people together and makes us feel good about being us and being social. From a caveman point of view, serotonin was the neurochemical that pulled tribes together and made our prehistoric relations feel they were contributing to the group and were safe as part of it. It's the chemical that says, 'It's good to be me and I'm glad I'm here'. That's awesome, we all want that. Give me the pill, Doc!

I understand why so many GPs get it wrong. They have 8 to 12 minutes to have a chat, do a few tests and see how they can help. It's impossible to connect with someone struggling with anxiety or depression in 8 to 12 minutes. Doctors are human. They have inner sea squirts too. Not being able to help must be a frustrating and uncomfortable feeling for someone with decades of schooling and a wealth of knowledge. Their inner sea squirt would be looking around for a way to feel better. Reaching for the Rx pad and dishing out the pill is a fairly tempting path of least resistance. At least they'd feel like they were doing something.

As for me, I took the Lexapro for about three weeks (they take at least that long to start working) and actually noticed a bit of an uptick in how I felt. My curiosity was really piqued now. Could I actually have been depressed? I did a bit of an audit of the different parts of my life. Family was good, I had a great circle of friends, and financially we were fine. Two parts of my world, however, were not where I wanted them to be: I was bored at work, and I was beefing up. As someone who is always pushing maximum density (I can get fat easily), I have a curious habit of comfort eating. In true sea squirt mode, my frustration with work was sending me down the path of scoffing chocolate-chip cookies for instant gratification and relief.

Around this time, I was doing boxing training, and my coach was a deep-thinking, complex man called Alan. He was like a cross between Mickey from the *Rocky* movies, Clint Eastwood and Yoda. I told him about the doctor and that I was uncomfortable with the diagnosis (this was a few years ago and my knowledge of mental health intricacies was nonexistent), as well as my life audit. He listened as I told him I needed to change my training plans and lose weight. Alan loved to challenge me with questions to ponder. He asked, 'Are you sad and frustrated because you are putting on weight, or are you putting on weight because you are sad and frustrated?'

We talked for a while, and Alan made me see that the problem was how I was looking at work. I was only noticing the boring bits and the monotony. I was telling myself a story that my job was boring. Because of that, I'd lost the spark that made me good at running businesses. Motivating people, leading, helping patients and bringing out the best in my team – these were the things I loved about running my business. I'd become so resentful of the boring parts that I'd started neglecting the parts of the job that I loved. We came up with a plan to compartmentalise the boring bits (put on your big-boy pants and just do it), and make sure I put my heart and soul into the bits I loved.

It was like I was the plant getting repotted. I got my mojo back and dropped some kilograms, and my team found another gear. I redid my schedule to have more time away from work and made sure that when I was there, I was there. Work got the better version of me once again. I went back to the doctor, and we decided to see how I went without chemical help.

Getting curious helped me change the lens I was viewing the world through. We are all making up stories about the world and our part in it. What Alan made me see was that if I was going to make up stories, I should at least make up stories that help.

That episode helped me realise the importance of being deliberate about how you look at things and how you show up, and to get curious about what you feel, think and do. I am forever grateful to that well-meaning GP – he started me down a five-year rabbit hole of learning about evolutionary biology, stress and the brain (and I still haven't found the bottom of it). But most of all, that episode taught me the importance of identifying the root cause of a problem, to get curious and reset how you look at it.

Let's get curious

- Where do you get 'pride from inside'?
- What parts of your life need to be repotted?
- Where in your life are you focusing on the symptoms and not the cause?

Chapter 15

Worry, let's see if that helps

> 'Worry is like a rocking chair: it gives you something
> to do but never gets you anywhere.'
> – Erma Bombeck

Some curious habits disguise themselves as signs you are a good and caring person. Take worry, for example. In the '90s, Baz Luhrmann told us that worry 'is as effective as trying to solve an algebra equation by chewing bubblegum'. But if worry, rumination and catastrophising are your habit loops of choice, it can be tricky to separate yourself from them once you are deep inside the cycle.

It might go something like this:

- **Cue:** My son didn't answer the phone.
- **Action:** Start to worry, panic and catastrophise about him being dead in a ditch.
- **Result:** Feel anxious and terrible – but at least it shows how much I care.

Dr Judson Brewer's book *Unwinding Anxiety* includes lots of actionable, easy-to-follow tips for getting out of anxious habit loops.

In it, he says: **'I had a lightbulb moment when I realized that one of the reasons so many people fail to see that they have anxiety is the way it hides in bad habits'.**

Feeling anxious can just be 'what you do'. It can feel so normal that you never stop and look for another option. It becomes part of your identity.

My friend Zoe has struggled with anxiety for years. Originally from Europe, she married an Australian and eventually moved her young family to Oz. Zoe has three kids and owns a very busy café, and has to deal with all the stress, staff problems and drama that go along with that. English is her second language, and between work, kids and cultural differences, she struggled to make genuine connections with her husband's friendship group. Feeling homesick and lonely, she became more highly strung and anxious. Already thin, she was losing weight, getting constant migraines that she was blaming herself for, and withdrawing from her friends. She was a tightly wound ball of nerves that could be set off by even the slightest trigger. Something had to change.

Zoe had a curious habit of being anxious and worrying that had become part of her identity. She saw herself as an anxious person. In Zoe's mind, being anxious had become a personality trait: 'My name is Zoe, I have brown hair, blue eyes and anxiety'.

I gave her a copy of my book *RESET*, and we talked about changing the story she was telling herself about anxiety and worry. We started working together to build a new, deliberate way of thinking that didn't involve blame, self-criticism or beating herself up. We had to change anxiety from being an identity trait back to a feeling – something that she *felt*, not who she *was*.

Feeling anxious is an emotion, NOT a character trait.

Our first step was to map out the triggers that sent her into an Old Brain shitstorm and turn them into **cues to get curious**. This first step was critical: she had to get really clear on what she felt in the moment when the worry started. With Zoe, it started with knots in the stomach, then progressed to clenching her hands and tightness in her shoulders. Often this would lead to debilitating migraines that would take her out of action for a day or two. Zoe described the over-riding feeling as tightness and constriction. She would wind herself up until her body tapped out and said 'enough' by knocking her out with a migraine.

With all the constriction and tightness she was feeling, her body was marinating in cortisol and adrenaline. When you're doing that, your New Brain goes offline and you can't think straight. The first thing we needed to do was get her biology sorted out.

I said to her, 'Imagine you had a button on the back of your hand and you could press it every time you got the trigger for anxiety. The button would calm the farm and you'd feel relaxed. Would you press it?'

'Absolutely', she replied. 'I'd be pushing it like a pensioner on the pokies.' She smiled, and I watched as her forehead relaxed and her hands unravelled.

I explained to her something I learned from Stanford neuroscience professor Dr Andrew Hubermann. He explained that we don't have a button to fix anxiety, but we do have something that does the same thing: our diaphragm!

You have 610 muscles in your body. One of them, the diaphragm, has a direct line to your hypothalamus, which is the part of your brain that controls your autonomic nervous system – things like your heart rate, your breathing and your blood pressure. The hypothalamus is like the Executive Assistant to your brain – it's the gatekeeper to the boss. The diaphragm is the one muscle that links straight to the hypothalamus. Engaging the diaphragm is proven to calm the nervous system and break the loop of a panic attack.

I also introduced Zoe to the Catch, WAIT, RESET concept. In my book *RESET* (written with co-author Ally Shorter), I described a strategy (based on cognitive behaviour therapy) I devised to help my clients with anxiety, rumination and catastrophising. Here's how it works:

- **Catch:** Catch the physical signs of stress. A racing heartbeat, knots in the stomach and sweaty palms are all signs of Dr Weekes's 'first fear' and we need to notice these with curiosity and acceptance – just like we do in the awareness part of habit SWAP.
- **WAIT:** WAIT stands for 'What Am I Thinking?' Why am I thinking this, and is it helping? (This is where curiosity comes in.)
- **RESET:** When a computer is overloaded and freezes, we press Control-Alt-Delete to do a RESET. We can do the same with our own brains by asking, 'What *can* I control? What are my alternatives? What should I delete? What deliberate habit loop can I select that will be more helpful?'

So, I asked Zoe to catch herself when she began feeling the initial cues of anxiety, then to breathe deeply through her nose into her stomach, so that her stomach extended out – that way, she'd know her diaphragm was engaged. Two or three really deep breaths is all it takes to get the Old and New Brains reconnected.

Then, I asked Zoe to WAIT. If you can understand **what you're thinking, why you're thinking it and whether or not it's helping**, you open up a whole world of curiosity that changes the way you look at a stressful situation.

The last thing I asked Zoe to do was a RESET. A RESET is a bit like the Serenity Prayer: **'God, grant me the serenity to accept the things I cannot change, courage to change things I can, and wisdom to know the difference'**.

So, Zoe had a few questions to ask herself:

- What can I control?
- What should I change? (What are my alternatives?)
- What must I delete?

Unlike a computer, Zoe didn't have a spinning circle that alerted her to a problem. What she did have were knots in the stomach and a feeling of constriction to give her a cue to get curious. And she now had a plan. She had a way to catch the first signs of worry, step out of her anxious habit loop, and RESET her system into a habit loop of curiosity and options. Her new habit loop would connect her Old and New Brains and allow her to deliberately make decisions rather than be stuck with her anxious defaults.

Remember in chapter 2 when I talked about the M1 motorway that was built next to the old highway between the Gold Coast and Brisbane? I used that analogy with Zoe, too. We called her new process, 'Building a new M1'.

A few weeks afterwards I got a text from Zoe: **'I have more lanes on my M1 now. Belly breathing is becoming a habit and I can now CATCH, WAIT and RESET when things get stressful. Thank you'**.

Let's get curious

- What habits are being 'triggered' by you feeling anxious?
- What is your first physical symptom that you are worrying?
- When could belly breathing help you?

Chapter 16

Feeding the beast

'Food is the most abused (and useless) anxiety medication
and exercise is the least utilised antidepressant.'
– Bill Phillips

Sophia is exhausted. Long workdays, coupled with the demands of being a single mum to three teenage boys, have her holding on by her fingertips. She is surviving on a combination of caffeine, adrenaline, wine and corn chips. The gym is a distant memory, and the only exercise she gets is a short walk to the kitchen for another sav blanc or some Doritos. She hasn't caught up with friends for months and hasn't been on a date in years, and her clothes have all gotten a bit snug.

Every Monday morning, Sophia wakes up at 5 a.m., tired after a handful of hours tossing and turning in bed, and vows that she's going to get her health and her life sorted. She thinks about making herself a healthy breakfast but realises she is short on time, and while herding the boys into the minivan to school, she grabs a muffin and guzzles a bucket of coffee. By 11 a.m., her workday has turned to shit, the boss is cranky (again), and her stress bucket is full. Sophia is chronically stressed and marinating in cortisol, and it's wreaking havoc on her eating and drinking habits.

No one has ever come home after a hard, stressful day at work and excitedly said, 'I really need a controlled portion of celery sticks and fat-free hummus'. This is not the way life works. After a big, stressful day, your brain and body feel uncomfortable. You want to feel better *now*!

The American Psychological Association has studied the most commonly used strategies for dealing with stress. What they found was that activities that fire up the brain's reward (dopamine) system – such as eating, drinking, shopping, watching TV, surfing the internet and playing video games – were top of the list.

When you feel uncomfortable, the sea squirt's answer is to find something to make you feel better. Booze, chocolate or double-cheese nachos work really well to provide instant gratification, but dopamine lollipops don't really help with the underlying chemistry of stress in the long term.

Psychiatrist Bill Phillips described food as the most misused and *ineffective* anxiety medication in the world. Eating sugar is like throwing petrol on an anxiety fire, but we do it anyway because our Old Brain is screaming for something that makes us feel good *now*.

We've talked a bit about the stress hormone cortisol. Along with adrenaline, this chemical prepares you to fight sabre-toothed tigers. You need energy to fight or run away, and cortisol signals the liver to liberate its glucose (sugar) stores, sending glucose into the bloodstream to give the muscles the energy they need to fight or flight. Good system, right? Ten thousand years ago, maybe, but today there are no sabre-toothed tigers, and no fighting or fleeing is required in most workplaces. So, what happens to this extra sugar in the system? Well, the extra sugar signals the pancreas to release the fat-storage hormone insulin. The liver doesn't detect sugars, but it does react to insulin by removing the sugars from the bloodstream, converting them to fat and storing them nearby as abdominal fat (visceral fat around the organs). This is the bad fat that has lots of negative health implications, and long-term stress plays a big part in why stressed people often have more visceral fat.

Adding comfort food into a high-sugar system equals fat gain.

The curious habit of using food for stress relief is creating a stress-sugar-insulin-fat cycle that is fuelling our obesity epidemic and making people like Sophia overweight.

Figure 16.1: The stress-sugar-insulin-fat cycle

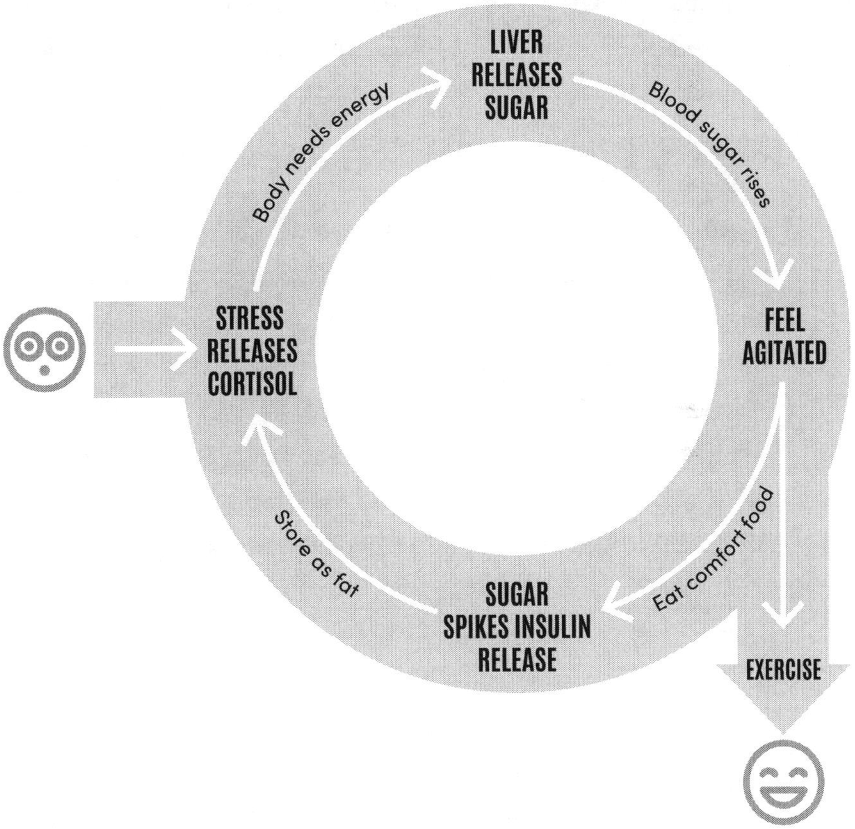

To fully understand the body's response to stress, you need to know that the human stress response is designed for a different environment.

I talked about this at the beginning of the book. Evolution takes thousands of years, and our stress response hasn't caught up to our modern lives. It's designed to be a short-term response. It's not optimised to help Sophia cope with life as a single mum with a cranky boss.

Because you need energy to fight sabre-toothed tigers, in times of stress your body is really sensitive to dropping sugar levels. Studies have shown that willpower – the ability to do the hard thing when it's the right thing to do – reduces when our sugar levels are falling. The post-sugar comedown feeds the stress beast and sends us back to the fridge in a vain attempt to appease our inner sea squirt and feel good again.

So, how do we step out of the cycle? How do we get off the roller-coaster of sugar and stress levels?

We need a deliberate habit loop. We need to SWAP out food (or drinking) as our response to a stressful situation and select a habit that will help us achieve our goals. This goes back to chapter 3 and my wrestle with Pepsi Max and chocolate-chip cookies. The goal I wanted to achieve was to feel calmer and less agitated. My default habit was to eat cookies, and the new deliberate habit loop I created was to do two minutes of belly breathing. I call belly breathing 'eating air burgers' because it calms the farm without the need for the calories and sugar rollercoaster.

The key is not to eat (especially sugar) until you are calm and the fight-or-flight response has subsided. Exercise is another great stress relief and has the extra bonus of speeding up the process by burning off the sugars.

Stress is a great thing: it helps us get things done and keeps us alive when we are under threat. By calming the fight-or-flight response, or doing some exercise, your sugars and insulin levels will return to normal.

If you are looking to drop a few pounds and improve your thought habits, think about it like this: exercise is the Batman of mental health and the Robin of weight loss.

Figure 16.2: Swapping Pepsi and cookies for air burgers

The 'what the hell' effect

Anyone who has ever tried to shed a few kilograms knows how hard it is to stick to new eating habits. You follow your new eating or exercise routine until a moment of temptation gets the better of you, and you stray. One errant biscuit turns into a whole packet, and in a heartbeat, you've just derailed your perfectly good weight-loss strategy.

Stress and exercise researcher Kelly McGonigal calls this the 'what the hell' effect. Her research has shown that if people think they have failed, their brain reasons that hey, they might as well go out with a bang.

It's not just eating the wrong thing that triggers the 'what the hell' effect in people on a diet. The grunt work to change habits takes effort and willpower. Unfortunately, stress, lack of sleep and feeling cranky can all put strain on your willpower muscle, like the infinite loop we talked about in chapter 2.

There's a sense of shame and disappointment that comes with the first sign of failure that can completely derail a new plan. One not very nice study rigged the subjects' scales to make people believe they had gained 2.5 kilograms (5 pounds) while trying to lose weight. Instead of strengthening their resolve to drop the kilograms, the poor dieters promptly turned to food to make their sea squirt happy and decrease the feelings of disappointment and guilt. What the hell?

I have a saying that 'No one disappoints me like I disappoint myself'. When I fail at a habit SWAP, my internal narrator chimes in with a quick 'I told you that would happen'. As we learned in the chapter on self-talk, this small version of yourself loves to be right. If the result isn't what you want, being right is the consolation prize for your internal nemesis.

There are a few tools we can use to keep on track and stop the 'what the hell' effect. One is to build in some fault tolerance. Make some room for small deviations from the plan and accept them as part of being human. Doing the pre-mortem discussed in chapter 3 can help with fault tolerance. Habits guru James Clear has a great example to build flexibility into his exercise routine: his rule is that 'he never misses two days in a row'. Having some fault tolerance for your new

Feeding the beast

habits can take the guilt and stress out of change and keep you on track while you build your new default habits.

As Sophia knows, stress can be a beast, and feeding the beast sugar, alcohol or caffeine is a curious habit. If she can get curious and deliberate about her desired rewards, she can SWAP habit loops and calm the farm while still fitting into her pants.

Let's get curious

- What dopamine lollipops are you feeding the beast?
- What is your new 'calm the farm' habit loop?
- How will you stop the 'what the hell' effect?

Chapter 17

Sober curious

'I drink to make other people more interesting.'
– Ernest Hemingway

'What do you mean you're *not* drinking? Have a beer, you pussy!'

For the last six months, I've heard versions of this from a heap of my mates. Booze is part of an unwritten Aussie social contract that is tough to break. The question is, is change possible with the help of curiosity?

After reading *Talking to Strangers* by Malcolm Gladwell (one of my all-time favourites), I got curious. One chapter explored the topic of alcohol-fuelled sexual assault on US college campuses. Gladwell described how, in legal cases involving sexual assault, it is often challenging to work out the truth about what happened. The reason: both people involved can barely remember.

So, what actually happens to the brain under the influence of booze? Gladwell found that the first areas of the brain affected are the frontal lobes – in other words, the New Brain. As we know, the New Brain is the bit that looks after your planning, simulates various outcomes and helps you choose the best option. Taking the frontal lobes offline with booze can turn unfunny people into comedians and shy wallflowers into rock stars – and can even get yours truly to dance. (No good comes from anyone witnessing me dance.)

As Gladwell points out, the first drink makes us less capable of making complicated decisions or handling competing demands. It hits our brain's reward centres and turns the amygdala – the 'fear centre' of the brain that tells us how to react to the world around us and whether we're in danger – down a notch.

In other words, we shed our inhibitions with our first couple of drinks because alcohol decreases the brain's ability to plan for possible outcomes (the New Brain goes offline) and downgrades the fear response. This is why drunk people do dumb shit. By the time we've had two to four drinks, the cerebellum starts to be affected, and we lose a bit of coordination – just a bit. Then – and this is what really got me interested – at around 0.08 percent blood alcohol level, the hippocampus (the memory centre) starts to struggle, and you lose a bit of short-term memory. You can still remember the old stories, you just can't make new ones when the hippocampus is offline. The hippocampus is right next door to the amygdala, deep in the Old Brain. There is a reason for this: it helps you remember when you do stupid (or dangerous) things and reminds you not to do them again. When you drink, your memory centre takes a holiday and is no good to you.

When I'm sober around people getting drunk, I notice they repeat themselves a lot. Repetition isn't a big problem to fellow pissheads because they, too, have forgotten the last time you told the story about your mate and the goat. When you take short-term memory offline, you become like a goldfish, and repetitive conversations remain endlessly fascinating – but to your sober friend… not so much.

At a blood alcohol level of 0.15 percent, the memory centre shuts down completely. It appears that memory loss is the free prize at the bottom of every vodka bottle. 'Great night! I can't remember exactly what happened, but I remember it was fun while my memory was still functioning.'

What's the point?

After reading *Talking to Strangers*, I had an epiphany: if I can't remember my night of drinking, what's the point?

In psychology and business, there is a concept called 'the law of diminishing returns'. It's when a specific course of action provides fewer benefits over time. To me, alcohol is a bit like that.

Suppose you were invited to spend a week on a superyacht in a beautiful tropical location, complete with movie stars and supermodels, with waiters serving you cocktails and mouth-watering food. The holiday would be spectacular. Fun, exciting people, scintillating conversation and lots of fun things to do. The only catch is, at the end of the trip, the organisers do a *Men in Black* trick and erase all memory of it. You get to keep the hangover, but the joyful memories are gone.

The question is, would you still want to go?

My answer is no – so why would I have a fifth drink?

London author Ruby Warrington is the founder of Club SÖDA NYC, an organisation that runs alcohol-free social events in New York City. Her book *Sober Curious* is changing people's relationship with booze.

As I write this, I have been (my version of) 'sober curious' for about six months now – after drinking every weekend for 30 years – and I love it! As part of my curiosity around alcohol use, I developed a concept called 'the window'. The window is the ideal alcohol level that allows maximum fun with no chance of the hippocampus going offline – so I try to keep my blood alcohol level below 0.08 percent.

Being 'boring'

One curious side effect of laying off the grog is being labelled 'boring'. It's ironic that you can be called 'boring' because you don't want to go out to the same pub, with the same people, to hear the same old stories over and over again, only to drink so much that you can't remember if you had fun or not. One mate of mine had the following reply when someone called him boring for not drinking: 'I was boring when I was drinking, it just didn't bother you because you were drunk'.

Humans hate the idea of being boring, but not as much as we hate the idea of not fitting in. In a drinking culture, the two together can make you feel like a social outcast if you don't partake.

Let's think about this in terms of habit loops:

· **Cue:** Catch up with friends.
· **Action:** Have a drink, followed by another... repeat.
· **Result:** Have lots of fun (until you don't), and feel like you belong as part of the group (except they're so drunk they probably don't remember what happened anyway).

Drinking is a great example of reward invariance. The reward (decreased inhibitions, social connection, and so on) gets the habit started, but eventually autopilot takes over and you do the routine anyway – even when the feel-good bonus is long gone.

The big problem with booze (and recreational drugs) is that the brain's 'bouncer' takes a vacation and lets any old person into the nightclub in your head. After drink four, you are stuck in your default habit loops – there is not a deliberate habit loop in sight. You want whatever you want, and you want it now. Proof: no sober person would eat a kebab at three in the morning.

Think back to Dave Mustaine. His default was to be angry and unreasonable, and he loved to get on the booze and drugs. But they didn't bring out the best version of this particular rock star.

Brian Slagel, the owner of Metal Blade Records, recalled in an interview:

'Dave was an incredibly talented guy, but he also had an incredibly large problem with alcohol and drugs. He'd get wasted and become a real crazy person, a raging megalomaniac, and the other guys just couldn't deal with that after a while. I mean, they all drank of course, but Dave drank more… much more. I could see they were beginning to get fed up of seeing Dave drunk out of his mind all the time.'

Booze goes in, truth comes out?

There is an Ancient Roman saying that goes: **'In vino veritas' (in wine there is truth)**.

There is a common belief that booze magnifies your default emotions. If your default is happiness, you'll be a happy drunk. If you have a tendency to be angry, you may get aggressive when drinking. There is definitely some truth to this idea, but it doesn't tell the whole story.

So much of what happens to people when drinking is dependent on context and environment. Psychologists and alcohol researchers Claude Steele and Robert Josephs developed what they call the 'alcohol myopia' theory. They found that alcohol narrows our feelings and thoughts to only those things that are right in front of us at that moment. In their words, alcohol causes 'a state of short-sightedness' whereby you can only focus on the things that are important *now*.

What the alcohol myopia theory suggests is that booze focuses us on our instant needs and blurs out the needs or wants we may have in the future. Drinking makes our immediate, dominant thoughts louder, and by decreasing inhibitions, it makes us more likely to voice them – whether that's a good idea or not. You may have a 'need' to tell your boss he's an arsehole when you are six Jägerbombs deep, but that doesn't make it a good idea.

A few years ago, when drinking was a bigger part of our lives, my wife Karen and I would occasionally go out for a night on the cans and she would 'turn' – meaning she would get uncharacteristically cranky, and direct her hostility towards me. She would go full 'Karen' on me. (Side note in her words: 'My name is Karen and I'm lovely. If I go full "Karen" on you, you deserve that shit!')

Living with me is not for the faint-hearted. The combination of a 98 percent extrovert with the energy levels of an Energizer Bunny and concentration span of a gnat is not a recipe you'd pick for a husband if you wanted a quiet life. Throw in my poor communication habits and a leaning towards 'some is good, more is better' (friends, food, work, exercise, fun…), and you get a bit of an idea of what my poor wife has had to deal with for the past 27 years. I try, but unfortunately I can sometimes get a bit excitable and not think about how my actions affect others (especially Karen). Losing your shit occasionally is understandable when you live with me.

Having drinks, and having the night deteriorate into an argument, is a curious habit. We sat down and had a talk about it, sober and in a calm state. I voiced my concern that I wasn't happy when a fun night out turned into an argument. She told me how my constant search for something exciting made her feel like I didn't care. We are both very agreeable people, and our default stress habit is to avoid conflict. The problem with avoidance is that the unresolved issue can become a dominant thought that bursts out from under the surface when the myopia of booze kicks in. The result was an uncharacteristic change from buried conflict to verbal combat.

Karen is Irish, and only once did she go full Conor McGregor on me (I totally deserved it). That particular evening ended with her 'turning' back and the two of us laughing about how much of an idiot I am. I dodged a bullet that time, but clearly something needed to change.

As we've discussed, being agreeable and avoiding conflict can be habits worth getting curious about. Even with people you love, it's possible to have unresolved issues and harbour resentments that stem from poor communication and not considering the other person's views. Agreeable people (like me and Karen) can tend to bury these feelings, and booze has a tendency to dig them up.

We needed a habit SWAP. The deliberate habit we came up with was to do a pre-mortem before any big night out. We would discuss anything that had been weighing on our minds. We used the pre-mortem as a safe opportunity to have a discussion in a cool and open state. Both of us used this time to voice any concerns, unresolved issues or criticism we had rolling around in our respective heads.

Karen read a quote that said: **'Every criticism is a *hope* in disguise'**.

I love that line! We decided that if we had criticisms of the other lurking in our heads we needed to voice them as a *hope* instead. Karen's hope was that I would improve my communication and be more considerate. By getting the hopes out in the open and having our discussions in a cold state, we no longer have arguments in a hot state after a few drinks.

Our personalities are made up of our defaults *and* the impulses we choose *not* to act on. 'In vino veritas', while offering some truth, is only telling part of the story.

By getting curious about what we get out of our habit loops, we can become aware of when the rewards go missing and make a plan (a pre-mortem) of what we are going to do instead.

Let's get curious

- What's your relationship with booze?
- What pre-mortem strategy would help you drink more deliberately?
- When the wine goes in, what 'truths' come out for you?

Chapter 18

Achievement addiction

'Not everything that is faced can be changed, but nothing
can be changed until it is faced.'
– James Baldwin

Josh really wanted to be a rock star. He loved music, had played piano
and guitar since he was a kid and dreamed of rocking out on stage to
a stadium full of adoring fans.

He was a very unpopular kid at school. Not in the angry, Dave
Mustaine sort of way – he just didn't quite fit in. Music offered him
a place to direct his energy and passion. Music gave him a little bit
of acceptance and something to strive for and care about. He would
get really anxious when he was performing, but he felt like being a
musician was the right call for him.

In his twenties Josh had a bit of success with his band, but he
never reached the dizzy heights of Dave Mustaine or Metallica. His
band sounded more like Blink-182 meets the blues. It had a modest
but enthusiastic local following.

Early on, Josh attached a lot of his happiness and self-worth to
how a gig went. If the crowd was a bit sparse, he would blame himself
and question whether he was any good. His sense of self-worth was

completely tied to how (he thought) the world saw him. People not showing up may have been because of bad weather or the fact that it was Tuesday night. Josh didn't see it this way. He described it as a true 'narcissistic injury' that would cut him to the core. He would take it as confirmation that he was unloveable, a shit singer, and that his tunes were no good. One bad gig would send his confidence spiralling into the toilet, with the corresponding uplift in anxiety. His self-worth became a rollercoaster attached to his interpretations of other people's opinions.

Fortunately, Josh grew up in a house that was very aware and informed about the mind and how it works. His dad, Lance, is a psychiatrist who taught at Harvard and obviously knows a thing or two about how the mind ticks. Josh was really struggling with feelings of anxiety around his rock star future, so his dad sorted out a therapist to help him deal with the racing mind and flocks of butterflies that had taken up permanent residence in his stomach. His dad was smart enough to realise that you can't do therapy on your own kids and, luckily, was never 'that dad'.

Josh says working through his 'stuff' with a great therapist allowed him a sense of acceptance. He found he needed the achievements a lot less as his anxiety decreased and he became happier.

Like most budding rock stars, there came a time when Josh realised he probably wasn't the next Jon Bon Jovi. He started to question if, and why, he wanted to be a rock star. The need for acceptance and validation was a big driver for Josh, and by his own admission, this was part of the reason he practised hard and gave it his all on stage. As he started getting curious about his thought habits, he actually lost a bit of his drive for music. Fortunately, this coincided with him being reacquainted with his other passion: psychology. The band broke up and Josh went back to school to learn a bit more about how we tick.

When I asked Josh which he loved more, the music or the adulation, he paused for a minute and really struggled to separate the two. He still loves music and has even rekindled his love of classical music. 'What I love is music', he eventually said. 'I love the creative part, and now the performance is no longer wrapped up in a need to be liked. I can play the music I love without the anxiety of being judged and the need for acceptance.'

Unhappy achievers

Achievement feels good. It's meant to. You get a little squirt of feel-good chemicals (dopamine and serotonin), and your brain sees this as a positive thing and decides, 'Let's do that again'. Achievement can be an addiction, especially when it is wrapped up in the swagger of being a rock star.

As we mentioned earlier, humans experience stress for two reasons: motivation and preservation. Stress gets you started, and stress makes you quit. If the levels of your stress hormones (cortisol and adrenaline) get too high, this makes you want to tap out and quit. Dopamine from achievement has a dampening effect on cortisol and actually lowers your stress hormones, allowing you to continue even when things get tough. When you're struggling with the stress of anxiety, a little dopamine lollipop from cheering fans is a great stress relief.

The problem with some people is that they need the achievement, but they don't register the good bits – they just move straight on to what's next. Josh calls these people 'unhappy achievers'. He says an unhappy achiever is a person who attaches their self-worth to the things they do. They believe their ability to be loved, validated and accepted – by themselves and by their tribe – is dependent on them 'doing' something.

Josh put it this way:

'These people may feel empty because of what their achieve-ments mean to them. For complex reasons, they feel that they have to achieve just to feel valuable or worthy. Achievements aren't a joy; they're a necessity. When someone is forced to achieve just to have any value, they can't stop. Stop achieving, and they stop being loveable. It's a terrible burden.'

A Harvard Graduate School of Education study found that young people identify 'achieving at a high level' as their highest priority. Other priorities like 'caring for others' and 'being a happy person (feeling good most of the time)' received fewer than half the votes as achievement. It's obvious from this that achieving is important – and it should be – but we can't let it be the sole driver of self-worth, connection and happiness.

If achieving is that important, it's not hard to see why the Western world is full of unhappy achievers. In her book *The Power of Vulnerability*, Dr Brené Brown explains that **people who have a strong sense of love and belonging believe they are worthy of love and belonging**. The problem is, many of us were taught to believe that we only get love and belonging if we do something that makes us worthy of it.

Placing contingencies on love and belonging is a curious habit:

- 'If I earn a million dollars, then I'll be loveable.'
- 'When I lose a few kilograms, then I will feel worthy of connection.'
- 'Once I fill stadiums and sing better than Bono, then I'll be happy.'

This kind of thinking will get you into trouble. It means the power to determine your self-worth is outside of yourself, and very often out of your control. As humans, we're all worthy of love and belonging just by being human. As Brown says, 'When you get to a place where you understand that love and belonging, your worthiness, is a birthright and not something you have to earn, anything is possible'.

Evolution and validation

The need to be liked and the search for validation through achievement are understandable curious habits. Both are evolutionary – they date back to a time when being alone was a death sentence. Being part of a crew and contributing to your tribe is so ingrained in our survival DNA that no matter how curious you get about it, it's not going to change. We need to belong.

If you have kids (or friends with kids), you'll have seen how they behave in an unfamiliar environment. They will leave their parents for a bit to explore, but every few moments they look back to make sure mum or dad is still watching. Kids want to be adventurous, and they want to be safe. Knowing the grown-ups are there gives them the courage to go further, be braver and try new things. Kids also love impressing their parents. 'Did you see me? Did you see me?' Like Crush, the super-cool sea turtle in *Finding Nemo*, little ones want validation when they do something that stretches their capabilities.

The curious habit of searching for validation is a well-worn brain pathway that stays with most people for life. Humans are designed to be insecure. We were designed to seek validation and support from the tribe, because if we got too confident and rocked out on our own, we got eaten by sabre-toothed tigers. Insecurity served us well on the plains of the Serengeti. It kept us connected to the safety of our tribe and open to help – good system. So, like most curious habits, when does seeking validation go from wanting to feel part of your tribe to something you need? When does your self-worth become dependent on what other people think of you?

In 1902, the sociologist Charles Horton Cooley wrote: **'I am not what I think I am, and I am not what you think I am. I am what I think you think I am'.**

Just read that again. If Cooley is right – and I suspect he is – we are wrapping up our identity and self-worth in what other people think of us. More accurately, we are wrapping our self-worth in what we *think* other people think of us.

Sometime in the '70s, the fledgling positive psychology movement decided that lacking self-esteem was to blame for everything, from kids failing geography to high crime rates. By the '80s and '90s we were dishing out seventh-place ribbons, not keeping score at kids' sporting events and giving everyone a participation trophy. We started validating mediocrity and giving kids a pseudo-squirt of achievement dopamine all in the name of protecting their self-esteem. To me this is the birthplace of entitlement.

As we discovered earlier, addiction rides on the dopamine express. The little squirts of dopamine make us repeat behaviours that got us there. If we get the reward, regardless of effort or results, doesn't that mean we are reinforcing neural pathways of entitlement that aren't helping?

In his work as a psychotherapist, Josh noticed a lot of really accomplished people who were spectacularly unhappy. He dug a little deeper and realised that these people *needed* the achievements to feel valid, but the feeling was fleeting, and then they felt a need to set off on another mission. Curious habit!

When we go back to our habit loops and B.J. Fogg's work on attaching a positive emotion to the desired habit (B.J.'s 'sunshine') we can see where the need for validation comes from. It feels good to be told you are doing a good job (or that your songs rock). Sea squirt 101 – let's do that again.

What changed for Josh was what belonging looked like – how he was going to contribute and why the world is a better place because he's in it. He now helps people every day in his psychotherapy clinic, raises his kids and helps unhappy achievers to look at their accomplishments through a different lens.

Looking for validation in all the wrong places

I have a curious habit of searching for validation from people who never give it. Getting good marks at school, running successful businesses and even writing books like this one are, at least partly, examples of me searching for validation (and I'm cool with that).

I can vividly remember the first time I got direct, obvious validation from my dad. I was 29 years old and living in the UK, and I flew my mum and dad over to celebrate the new millennium with us. We were playing golf overlooking Brighton in the south of England. We started talking about how well my Specsavers business was going, and I casually said that I'd just gotten lucky and was in the right place at the right time. Dad stopped walking, put his hand on my shoulder and turned me around to look at him. 'It wasn't luck. You have done a great job, you've worked hard, built an amazing business and I'm really proud of you.' It meant a lot; I may have teared up a little bit and the two of us had a big hug.

Dad grew up in a time when men were not taught much about emotions. They were told to get on with it and soldier on. Giving (or getting) compliments was not something he had much experience with. There was never any doubt that he cared, he just showed it in more subtle ways. He showed he cared by always being there for me (and he still is). He was the goal umpire for my footy team, and drove me to cricket and sat around in the stinking hot summer sun to watch me get out for a hard-fought eight runs (on a good day). Saying it straight out was not his style, which is why what he said to me on that day meant so much and the memory is still so vivid.

We all need validation in one way or another. Validation is our signal that the tribe values our contribution – super-important. One person not valuing us might not feel so bad, but when that one person is perceived as being high up the pecking order, validation becomes more desirable. It makes sense: we are primates, and just like with baboons and gorillas, it's a pretty wise move to stay on the alpha's good side.

Trying something new and getting criticism from other people rarely feels good, and if you let it, criticisms can derail confidence and stop you doing the thing you really want. We all have buttons that fire up our self-doubt monster. When someone pushes that button, it stings, and our sea squirt goes running for the safety of the status quo.

Curiosity removes the power of criticism to derail your confidence. I have three questions I like to ask myself when dealing with criticism:

1. Is the criticism valid and, if so, how can I improve?
2. Who is it coming from?
3. What is the person's intent?

If the criticism is valid, thank the person for it and get curious about how to improve.

The second question is where you need to be particularly curious. In a world of keyboard warriors and armchair experts, it's easy to get a flat tyre on your confidence car if you listen to everyone's opinion.

Theodore Roosevelt's 'man in the arena' quote is a good place to start when assessing where any criticism is coming from:

> 'It is not the critic who counts; not the man who points out how the strong man stumbles, or where the doer of deeds could have done them better. The credit belongs to the man

who is actually in the arena, whose face is marred by dust and sweat and blood; who strives valiantly; who errs, who comes short again and again, because there is no effort without error and shortcoming; but who does actually strive to do the deeds; who knows great enthusiasms, the great devotions; who spends himself in a worthy cause; who at the best knows in the end the triumph of high achievement, and who at the worst, if he fails, at least fails while **daring greatly**, so that his place shall never be with those cold and timid souls who neither know victory nor defeat.'

I first heard this quote in a Brené Brown TED Talk, and I have since read her book *Daring Greatly*. Both the former US President and my guru Texan TED Talker are communicating one simple message: **If you are not out there trying, I don't give a shit about your opinion**.

Or, as Tim Minchin says, 'Opinions are like arseholes, in that everyone has one'. He goes on to say that, unlike arseholes, your own opinions need to be thoroughly examined.

The last question we need to think about relates to the person's intent. There are a lot of people who have the misguided and curious habit of blowing out other people's candles in the hope it will make theirs shine brighter.

The German word 'schadenfreude' means taking joy from someone else's misfortune. Any whiff of schadenfreude automatically puts a big cross next to that person's feedback.

As I said earlier, everyone needs to feel like they are contributing to the tribe, so searching for validation is not such a curious habit. Searching for validation from people who aren't in the arena and get joy from other people's misfortune is definitely something to get curious about.

As I've mentioned before, there is an old saying that 'Other people's opinions of you are none of your business'. Find mentors you trust and who have good intentions, speak to others in the arena, and most of all, catch yourself doing things well. Like B.J. Fogg's sunshine, getting joy and validation from your wins is a great way to reinforce positive habits. If you can notice your achievements without your self-worth being attached to the results, you'll thrive from a place of abundance.

Let's get curious

- Are you putting self-worth on the other side of achievement?
- When do you catch yourself doing something well?
- Whose opinion do you value?

Chapter 19

Dodging the tough chat

'When we avoid difficult conversations, we trade
short-term discomfort for long-term dysfunction.'
– Peter Bromberg

Whether you call them 'curly conversations', 'rumbles' or 'constructive chats', it doesn't matter – the very thought of having a difficult conversation sends most of us straight into sea squirt mode. Our Old Brain senses danger, and we'd rather do anything than cause conflict that could potentially see us kicked out of our tribe.

I have a curious habit of rehearsing future difficult conversations in my head over and over. Figuring out what to say in a tricky situation is perfectly understandable and could even be a good idea; rolling those fictitious future conversations around in your head but never actually *having* them is a curious habit.

We are all familiar with rumination – that nagging voice in your head that keeps going over difficult imaginary conversations. The word 'ruminate' comes from the Latin word for chewing cud, which is the digestive habit of cattle where they grind up, swallow, regurgitate and then rechew their food. These conversations you are having with yourself are noise: unwanted, annoying chatter that doesn't clarify or teach. Rumination strengthens unwanted neural pathways, increasing toxic stress and making it even less likely you'll have the courage to say the thing that needs to be said. Negative bias, which we learned about in chapter 1, also skews the fictional outcome towards a lousy result.

In chapter 11, we talked about 'noise-cancelling habits' – things you do once and they eliminate a bunch of other distractions. What if we could get rid of this pointless rumination by simply having the tough chat?

As a leader, I often struggled to give feedback to certain staff members who weren't performing. I talked to a friend and mentor of mine, mindset expert Danny Ginsberg, and asked him how to get better at having tough conversations at work.

His advice? 'Just have the chat!' Whenever one of his managers had a problem with a team member, his first question was always, 'Does that person know that they are causing problems?' Have the conversation or provide the feedback from a good place, and trust that it will be heard that way, too. Challenging conversations are never as hard as they are in your head.

Conflict is OK, combat is not

Feedback queen Georgia Murch works with corporations all over the world to improve their communication and make their teams better at conflict. She says conflict is OK, but combat is not. When it comes to stressful interactions where there may be conflict, Murch has a great observation: **'People hear your content but they smell your intent'**.

Her advice is to be **crystal clear about your intent**. Having your statistics on point and spending hours rehearsing the perfect way to communicate your message doesn't help if you haven't worked out what you want to achieve with the conversation. You need to know your intent.

I recently asked Georgia why people avoid difficult conversations, and her number-one reason was *fear*. 'Makes sense,' I said, 'but fear of what?'

She said that as soon as people start identifying what fears they have associated with giving feedback, that's actually when they get to unpack the fears and work out whether they're true or not.

She went on to explain that many people believe giving constructive feedback could damage relationships. We'd rather keep things nice. But in her 20-plus years working with organisations, Murch has rarely seen a case where people giving respectful feedback has led to a relationship going south. The worst-case scenario is that the relationship stays the same, while the upside is that the relationship improves because of increased trust and respect. If you know that this other person is going to give you information in a respectful way, you can trust their intent and have a two-way conversation.

'But I might upset them'

According to Murch, the second most common reason for avoiding the tough chat is fear of an emotional reaction. What if I upset them and they cry? Avoiding a conversation that might upset someone is letting your sea squirt run the show. Some people arc up and get aggressive when you initiate difficult conversations with them. I don't like that either – my inner sea squirt is going to dodge that conversation, too.

Georgia says dodging difficult conversations because you are concerned about another person's emotional reaction means **placing your comfort ahead of that person's growth**. As we learned in a previous chapter, getting comfortable with discomfort is necessary if we want to get curious about our habits. We can listen to our inner sea squirt, but it doesn't get a vote in what we do.

How people have reacted to tricky conversations you've had in the past has a big influence on how much fear you experience. If you have a history of giving feedback to someone who cries, you are way less likely to want to deal with that again.

Mellody Hobson is co-CEO of Ariel Investments and the first woman of colour to be chairperson of a Fortune 500 company (Starbucks). She says she doesn't have time to deal with emotional responses, but understands the importance of feedback where it's needed.

In an episode of the podcast *WorkLife with Adam Grant*, she told the story of getting some harsh but constructive feedback from one of her mentors: Hall-of-Fame basketball champion and former US senator Bill Bradley. He sat her down and explained that 'if she wasn't careful, she could be a ball-hog'. She went on to explain, 'I remember sitting there and telling myself, "Don't cry". I was certainly second-guessing myself and thinking, "Why is he saying this to me?" It didn't feel very good, but I also thought to myself at the time, "If I cry, he won't ever give me feedback again"'.

In the podcast, Hobson explained that nobody wants to have to sit there and put someone back together after giving them feedback. She left the encounter with Bradley (dry-eyed) thinking of ways she could put his advice into practice.

Hobson said that feedback doesn't always come wrapped in a pretty box with a bow. When you're receiving feedback, you have to try to separate the way in which the feedback is delivered from the message that it is delivering. But if you are giving feedback, make sure you are clear about your intent and be prepared to go back and forth, conversation-style. Georgia Murch describes effective feedback as a 'dance' or a 'tennis rally'. It takes effort and intent from both sides, coupled with open minds and ears for listening. When done well, feedback can actually unite teams and take the resentment out of our relationships.

Let's get curious

- What conversations do you ruminate over? Can you just have the chat?
- How can you make your intent clearer?
- If you are a leader, does potential discomfort stop you giving feedback?

Chapter 20

Phoning it in

'I have a very strong feeling that the opposite of love
is not hate – it's apathy. It's not giving a damn.'
– Leo Buscaglia

The documentary *Freakonomics* contained a story on what makes a good parent. They looked at socio-economic status, age and the amount of time the parents spent with the kids, and they couldn't find any correlation between these factors and good parenting.

What they did find, however, is that every good parent bought a parenting book. They didn't even have to read the book. The fact that they cared enough to buy the book made them a better parent.

Parents need to care, and to show they care. It's no different from business leaders. If you are going to lead teams, caring is the most crucial trait. You must care about your people, care about workplace culture and care about the example you are setting for your staff.

When I sold my final optometry business after 27 years of running busy practices, I was ready to embark on the next adventure. Before I set off on my mission to RESET how people deal with stress, I thought it might be a good idea to look back at those years, get curious and do a stocktake on what I'd learned.

I looked at the times when my businesses were at their best and I was happiest. There were years when we set national records, innovated and broke barriers that allowed the business to go to the next level. In these years, I inspired people to become leaders themselves. In other years, I trod water.

What was the difference? It hurts me to admit it, but the secret sauce was how much I cared!

In the years when I, the leader, was giving it my all, the business boomed. But in the times when I was phoning it in, we floundered. We lacked connection with our customers, and we went through the motions. I was the leader, and if I didn't care (and show I cared), why would anyone else?

The weird thing, looking back, is that the times I enjoyed most were also the hardest. Enjoying the journey and striving was the most fun, even though the challenges were significant. The 14-hour days were tough at the time, but I look back on them with pride.

Phoning it in – whether it's in work, sport, relationships or crocheting bowling-ball bags – is a curious habit.

A leader must care and show they care. Every action is noted by your team, and every effort is a vote for the type of leader you wish to be and the culture you want to lead.

Stress can be a threat, or stress can be a challenge. Leaders who care help stress be a challenge. Great leaders know how to navigate for their teams when they come to the fork in the stress road. By treating stress as a challenge, organisations embrace difficult situations, find better solutions and derive pride from their accomplishments. When stress is a threat, we become defensive, close-minded and selfish.

Business leaders, like parents guiding teens through tough times, are there to help. A leader's job is to make the people around them feel safe and able to do their jobs to the best of their abilities. Should leaders read parenting books? Possibly not… but they do need to care enough to learn. Curiosity and a willingness to learn are vital if you are going to lead, particularly in an age of innovation. Bill Gates reads 50-plus books a year, and a lot of them are on leadership. He's curious and innovative, and is always looking for a way to improve how the world works. He cares.

I think you can break the CARE factor down into four traits:

1. **Consistent:** When people show up differently every day, it stresses their workmates out and increases anxiety.
2. **Agile:** Leaders need to be able to shift direction and change when necessary. Understanding the habit SWAP can help you become more flexible.
3. **Robust:** You can't lead if you are no good at stress. Being resilient is essential for leading productive teams.
4. **Empathetic:** Understanding others and being able to take their perspectives into account is an essential part of the CARE factor.

When I do Stress RESETs in an organisation, one of the key factors is building the 'safety of the tribe'. It's up to the leader to make people feel secure. The leader has to CARE (and show they care) to make the people around them feel safe. When we feel safe, stress is a challenge. When leaders don't show they CARE, stress is a threat and teams become defensive, selfish and dumb.

Phoning it in is a curious habit. Not caring may decrease some stress and help you feel better in the short term, but it always bites you in the arse eventually. Any long-term habit needs the CARE factor.

Let's get curious

- What does 'phoning it in' look like to you?
- Have you ever stopped caring? Did it help?
- What CARE factor trait do you need to work on?

Wrapping it up

We all have curious habits – things we think, feel and do that no longer serve us. If you want to change these habits, *don't* do it from a place of scarcity, lack or disappointment. Start by working out what you want and striving from a place of gratitude, acceptance and purpose. Get clear on what the best version of you looks like and change because you want to, not because you have to.

Real change comes from getting curious.

As this book draws to a close, I'd like to do a two-part thought experiment that one of my mentors, leadership expert Cam Schwab, taught me.

Suppose you could go back in time and talk to yourself half a lifetime ago. For me, that would be the 25-year-old version of myself. And before you think it, I am not going to cliché up and ask what advice you would give the younger version of yourself. The first part of the thought experiment is this: **What would you thank the younger you for?**

What decisions did they make that got you here? What sacrifices did they make? What did they learn that set the foundation for who you are today? What would you say to the younger version of yourself to show them how grateful you are?

We talked in chapter 9 about living in the gap between where you are and who you want to be. Gratitude is a way to bridge that gap. It's a way of building on the gains you've already made and using them as a platform for what's next.

I'm grateful for the hard work and tenacity my younger version showed when a few things got tough. I'm grateful that he sorted his shit out when he was a stoner and his brain and mental health went off the rails. I'm grateful he (and, more importantly, Karen) went through IVF and had a beautiful daughter who has grown into a wonderful young lady. That young version of me took some risks, messed some things up (think Taiwanese Jellyfish Chairs) and learned some cool shit. I'm glad he was curious enough to find mentors, read books and look for ways to constantly improve. I'm grateful he fought for his marriage when it looked like it might not make it, and I'm really grateful he tried to be a better husband (still working on that one). It took a while, but I'm glad he learned that if some is good, more isn't always better (another work in progress).

Gratitude is about the past. There will always be some regrets about opportunities lost or poor decisions made. Regrets are life's school fees – the price you pay for the lessons learned that got you to where you are. This isn't toxic positivity – some of those lessons sucked. It's about acceptance of the past and learning not to repeat the stuff that doesn't align with the truest version of you.

The second part of the thought experiment is to time-travel the same amount forward, and ask: **What would the older you thank the current you for?**

What things would 75-year-old Luke thank current Luke for? He would thank me for staying fit and looking after those knees. He'd thank me for taking up Pilates and finally learning how to putt. The old bloke would hopefully appreciate that I found new mentors and stayed curious. He would thank me for being generous and helping lots of other people, and making him proud of the contributions he has made in his 75 years. Future me would thank me for building bridges and staying connected with the people I love and who love me back.

I hope future me will also thank current me for being brave enough to have the tough chats, remaining honest, and enjoying the view from the top of the mountain while embracing the journey, both up and down. He'll thank me for getting more sleep, fasting, laying off the carbs and staying sober curious. He will be proud of me for wrestling with imposter syndrome and still managing to write books and run workshops that help people. He will thank me for doing the grunt work and changing the default habit loops that were no longer helping.

In the introduction, I quoted Marshall Goldsmith, who said: **'What got you here won't get you there'**.

My wish is that future me will thank current me for sticking to my identity goals and remaining curious, creative and generous.

I hope your future you will thank you for reading this book and getting curious about your habits. If they can do that, current me will be really happy.

Sources and further reading

Achor, S (2011). *The Happiness Advantage: The Seven Principles that Fuel Success and Performance at Work.* Random House UK.

Ariely, D (2010). *Predictably Irrational: The Hidden Forces that Shape Our Decisions.* HarperCollins.

Brewer, J & Kabat-Zinn, J (2018). *The Craving Mind: From Cigarettes to Smartphones to Love—Why We Get Hooked and How We Can Break Bad Habits.* Yale University Press.

Brewer, J (2021). *Unwinding Anxiety: Train Your Brain to Heal Your Mind.* Random House UK.

Brown, B (2016). *Daring Greatly: How the Courage to Be Vulnerable Transforms the Way We Live, Love, Parent, and Lead.* Penguin UK.

Brown, B (2021). *Atlas of the Heart: Mapping Meaningful Connection and the Language of Human Experience.* Vermillion.

Clear, J (2018). *Atomic Habits: An Easy and Proven Way to Build Good Habits and Break Bad Ones.* Random House UK.

David, S (2017). *Emotional Agility: Get Unstuck, Embrace Change and Thrive in Work and Life.* Penguin UK.

DeSanti, M (2019). *New Man Emerging: An Awakening Man's Guide to Living a Life of Purpose, Passion, Freedom & Fulfillment.* Waterside Productions.

Duhigg, C (2013). *The Power of Habit: Why We Do What We Do, and How to Change*. Random House UK.

Dweck, C (2017). *Mindset: Changing the Way You think To Fulfil Your Potential*. Little Brown.

Eyal, N (2022). *Indistractable: How to Control Your Attention and Choose Your Life*. Bloomsbury.

Fogg, BJ (2021). *Tiny Habits: The Small Changes That Change Everything*. Random House UK.

Fung, J (2016). *The Obesity Code: Unlocking the Secrets of Weight Loss*. Scribe Publications.

Gilbert, D (2006). *Stumbling on Happiness*. HarperCollins Publishers.

Gladwell, M (2020). *Talking to Strangers: What We Should Know about the People We Don't Know*. Penguin UK.

Goggins, D (2018). *Can't Hurt Me: Master Your Mind and Defy the Odds*. Lioncrest Publishing.

Grant, A (2021). *Think Again: The Power of Knowing What You Don't Know*. Random House UK.

Hardy, B (2018). *Willpower Doesn't Work: Discover the Hidden Keys to Success*. Hachette Books.

Hari, J (2019). *Lost Connections: Uncovering the Real Causes of Depression – and the Unexpected Solutions*. Bloomsbury.

Hari, J (2022). *Stolen Focus: Why You Can't Pay Attention*. Bloomsbury Publishing.

Irvine, WB (2021). *The Stoic Challenge: A Philosopher's Guide to Becoming Tougher, Calmer, and More Resilient*. W W Norton & Company.

Kross, E (2021). *Chatter: The Voice in Our Head and How to Harness It*. Random House UK.

McCubbin, A (2021). *Why Smart Women Make Bad Decisions: And How Critical Thinking Can Protect Them.* Major Street Publishing.

McGonigal, K (2012). *Maximum Willpower: How to Master the New Science of Self-Control.* Pan Macmillan UK.

McGonigal, K (2013). *The Willpower Instinct.* US.

McGonigal, K (2021). *The Joy of Movement: How Exercise Helps Us Find Happiness, Hope, Connection, and Courage.* Penguin Group.

McKay, A (2021). *You Don't Need an MBA: Leadership Lessons That Cut Through the Crap.* Major Street Publishing.

Milkman, K (2022). *How to Change: The Science of Getting from Where You Are to Where You Want to Be.* Random House UK

Panda, S (2018). *The Circadian Code: Lose Weight, Supercharge Your Energy and Sleep Well Every Night.* Random House UK.

Shetty, J (2020). *Think Like a Monk: How to Train Your Mind for Peace and Purpose Everyday.* Harper Collins Publishers.

Silver, Dr A (2021). *The Loudest Guest: How to Change and Control Your Relationship With Fear.* Major Street Publishing.

Sullivan D & Hardy, Dr B (2021). *The Gap and the Gain: The High Achievers Guide to Happiness, Confidence, and Success.* Hay House.

Weekes, Dr C (1995). *Self Help for Your Nerves.* HarperCollins.

von Hippel, W (2018). *The Social Leap: How and Why Humans Connect.* Scribe Publications.

About the author

Luke Mathers is positive of two things:

- You can't LEAD if you are no good at STRESS; and
- The first person you have got to LEAD is YOURSELF.

He is the author of *Stress Teflon*, *RESET* and now *Curious Habits*. Twenty-eight years of running successful businesses have taught him that stress isn't going away any time soon. If you want to have better health, relationships and success, you need to get good at stress.

As one of the original directors of Specsavers in Australia, Luke was part of the biggest retail roll-out in Australia's history – 100 stores in 100 days. His practice was the biggest in the country and set global records that were previously unheard of.

Luke retired for the first time at age 31. After transforming his UK Specsavers practice (increasing turnover by 350 percent in just three years), Luke returned to Australia to relax and put his feet up. It wasn't long before he realised he missed something... stress!

Helping people get curious about their habits and reset stress is his mission. Through his keynote speeches, workshops and coaching he helps people turn threats into challenges. As the book says, 'It's good being you when stress doesn't stick'.

Acknowledgements

As I said earlier in the book, I'm not the first to think that everything has been thought before. This book has been a curation, a gathering of information from generations of smart people – from B.F. Skinner to B.J. Fogg, Brené Brown to Judson Brewer, and Johann Hari to Benjamin Hardy and Malcolm Gladwell. Books are a big part of my life, and I am so grateful to all the wonderful authors whose books have moulded my take on the world. This book has adapted the recipes of others and hopefully pulled the good bits into one good dish. I am forever grateful to those authors who inspired and taught me.

To Mick Zeljko, my guru of all things neuro and my favourite person to bounce ideas off.

Georgia Murch, Paige Williams, Lynne Cazaly and Amy Silver, you all taught me to be brave and how to have tough conversations from a kind place. To all my coaching clients, I'm convinced I learn more from you than you do from me.

'You can't polish a turd', they say, but my editor Brooke Lyons can find a good idea buried in my combinations of mixed metaphors and poor grammar, and thanks to her polishing skills, this book is actually readable. I will miss our chats. To Lesley Williams at Major Street, you and your stable of authors are all inspiring humans. Thank you for entrusting me with the *Your Next Read* podcast and encouraging me to write this book. I am beyond proud to be part of the Major Street team.

Lastly, and most importantly, to my beautiful wife Karen (you are the string on my helium balloon), and daughter Chloe: your ability to tolerate me when I need to bounce half-baked ideas around is a true measure of love. Thank you for giving me space when I needed it and pulling me out of rabbit holes that weren't helping.

To *you*, the reader, if you got to here I am truly grateful and hope you have a new love of and curiosity about your habits.

Thank you for sticking with me until the end. It's been emotional!

in

linkedin.com/in/luke-mathers-speaker

@lukemathers_official

f

@lukemathers_official

✉

luke@lukemathers.com.au

For enquiries about having Luke speak at your
conference go to lukemathers.com.au

Be better with business books

MAJOR STREET

We hope you enjoy reading this book. We'd love you to post a review on social media or your favourite bookseller site. Please include the hashtag #majorstreetpublishing.

Major Street Publishing specialises in business, leadership, personal finance and motivational non-fiction books. If you'd like to receive regular updates about new Major Street books, email info@majorstreet.com.au and ask to be added to our mailing list.

Visit majorstreet.com.au to find out more about our books (print, audio and ebooks) and authors, read reviews and find links to our Your Next Read podcast.

We'd love you to follow us on social media.

in linkedin.com/company/major-street-publishing

f facebook.com/MajorStreetPublishing

○ instagram.com/majorstreetpublishing

▶ @MajorStreetPub